CW01650017

MAKE MORE MONEY FROM YOUR IDEAS

MAKE MORE MONEY FROM YOUR IDEAS

THERÉSA LÜTGE-SMITH

Struik Book Distributors
(A member of the Struik Group (Pty) Ltd)
32 Thora Crescent
Wynberg, Sandton

Reg. No. 63/06481/07

First published in 1994

© Struik Book Distributors 1994
Text © Therésa Lütge-Smith 1994

All rights reserved. No part of this publication may be reproduced, stored in a retrieval system, or transmitted, in any form or by any means, electronic, mechanical, photocopying, recording or otherwise, without the permission of the copyright owner/s.

Editors: Hilda Hermann and Wenda Pace

Page make-up and typesetting: Suzanne Fortescue, Struik DTP
Reproduction: Hirt & Carter (Pty) Ltd
Printed and bound by CTP Book Printers, Parow

ISBN 1-875015-01-9

*Dedicated to my husband, Gary,
and sons, Bryan, Paul, Robin
and Matthew.*

Dedicated to my husband, Gary, and sons Bryan, Paul, Robin and Matthew.

Contents

INTRODUCTION

■

South Africa is characterized by a mixture of diverse cultures and attitudes, poverty and prosperity, unrest and tranquillity. It is a combination of First World and Third World economies.

While large sections of the population are frantically reassessing their futures in this country there is a group of individuals who have identified the vast number of opportunities available in an unsaturated but rapidly growing urban market – both locally and throughout Africa.

What determines whether a country prospers with the First World or stagnates in the Third World? The answer to this question can be illustrated by way of the South African combination of (non-political) conservatism on the one hand, and liberalism on the other. While the latter group 'profit-seek' by investing time and money to produce more goods and services for the people, the former 'rent-seek', depleting resources to obtain more of what already exists and causing the economic pie to shrink. They make money, not by producing more wealth, but by protecting or redistributing existing wealth in their favour. To thrive, rent-seeking must not dominate profit-seeking.

The roots of First World prosperity exist in the profit-seeking attitude of many South Africans. This is manifested in the spirit and energy of the street vendor, the taxi-driver, the backyard motor mechanic and the sphaza owner; it can also be found in the thriving housing market and the demand for excellence in education. Clearly, South Africa needs more wealth – more jobs, more businesses, more trade and higher levels of production. In short, every effort should be made to stimulate national and foreign buying and make South Africa a good place to do business. Local and overseas financiers should be encouraged to invest in the emerging South African market, to support projects such as new housing developments, to establish factories, to set up export-import companies and to bank their assets *here*.

Economic upliftment will go hand-in-hand with an improved climate for entrepreneurial endeavours and economic self-sufficiency. If the economic climate of profit-seeking prospers, the country will prosper. If rent-seeking dominates, however, decline will be imminent.

For profit-seeking and wealth creation to overtake rent-seeking and wealth protection, prosperity, non-racial democratic principles and a capitalist economy *must* be promoted actively.

But apart from profit-seeking, there is another factor which is motivating individuals to enter the world of entrepreneurship: people are becoming increasingly dissatisfied with salaries that cannot keep pace with the rate of inflation. It is said that 'necessity is the mother of invention', and this is especially true in adverse economic times, when people who are ordinarily content with their living standards, are motivated to develop their entrepreneurial talents, either in the formal or informal sector. Consequently, more and more employees are quitting the corporate environment and, using their experience and skills, turning to self-employment.

This prospective workforce, together with the declining employment opportunities, emphasizes the urgent need for both large and small business development in South Africa. People must be encouraged to seek alternative forms of employment actively, either by selling items they have made or bought, or by selling their skills and services. This, however, requires an ability to generate creative ideas, and identify profitable opportunities and resources through which they can be developed.

Industry is also waking up to the fact that the smaller fish in the expansive business pond can provide products and services with a competitive advantage. As a result, more and more entrepreneurs are coming to the fore with great ideas. Technological advances are allowing small enterprises to conduct their business in ways that only large institutions with significant capital investments previously could. Futurists identify these trends in industries such as entertainment, education, health care (mental, physical and cosmetic), spiritual enhancement/religion, ethnically-related concepts, self-discovery, financial security, and personal safety and security.

Large companies are beginning to hire small businesses to do things that were done previously on an in-house basis, and, in this way, are creating opportunities for the small business sector to increase its contribution to the national economy.

Nevertheless, a supportive environment for the development of a business opportunity is dependent on many factors, such as financing, training and development, available infrastructure, legal restrictions in the economic sphere and the current economic policy of authorities.

Deregulation, for example, is a boost to the private sector as activities that were once prohibited are now accepted. The growth in the number of sphaza shops, for example, with their increasing turnover and expanding product ranges is a multi-million rand industry. Another illustration of the benefits of easing restrictions is the growth of home-based businesses, in particular those that operate as a 'light industry', such as welding, carpentry and motor vehicle repairs.

Almost everyone has an idea that they think will make money. How often have you heard the remark, 'You're so talented, why don't you ...' or, 'Wouldn't it be a good idea if ...' and, 'That idea can earn you a lot of money ...'? The success rate, however, is not as high as it could be because small business owners have a general lack of business knowledge and often neglect to implement long-term planning. Some of these ideas *do* get to the planning stage, but still lack the essential ingredient for attracting capital: they don't make economic sense!

The key is *profit*. If an idea can't or won't generate profit, it doesn't make economic sense. Money can be spent on all the things a business needs to get going (rent, equipment, employees, suppliers and vendors etc.) but eventually that money will run out – *unless* there is a formula to make a profit.

Many would-be entrepreneurs think finding a new or better way to do something is a good reason to go into business, but this isn't always the case. Finding a way to make a *profit* is a good reason to go into business. Market research, together with intuition, is also an essential part of long-term planning in order to establish whether there is a sufficient demand for a particular service or product. Operating a small business is a very practical, but challenging occupation. It involves desire, theoretical knowledge, practical experience, hard work, and occasionally elements of luck.

Thus, while the aspirant entrepreneur may have every possible reason – motivation, resources and a good marketable idea – to explore self-employment, he or she may find it difficult to choose a business, and may lack the experience and knowledge concerning financing, starting and running a potentially profitable enterprise.

All of these aspects will be dealt with in *Make More Money From Your Ideas*. The book includes a self assessment analysis, information on how to go about choosing a business, costings, marketing options, financing, creating a business plan, and personnel and legal considerations.

But most importantly, this book presents a wealth of information on generating, assessing and developing ideas and concepts, with the aim of turning them into viable and profitable businesses.

THERÉSA LÜTGE-SMITH

CHAPTER

1

GENERATING IDEAS

■

23 WAYS TO GENERATE IDEAS

■

Each year an oak tree produces enough acorns to populate a good-sized forest, yet from these bushels of seeds perhaps only one or two acorns will become a tree. The squirrels destroy most of them and the hard ground beneath the tree doesn't give the few remaining seeds much chance for a start.

So it is with ideas. Very few actually bear fruit. Ideas are highly perishable. If we are not on guard, the squirrels (negative thinking people and our own lack of confidence) will destroy most of them. Ideas require special handling from the time they are conceived until they can be transformed into practical ways for achieving objectives and making money.

Fear of failure is one of the greatest inhibitors of natural creativity, and yet, every successful innovator has failed – often. It's almost comforting to know that absolute perfection is unattainable, but this means that there is always room for improvement.

Most successful people know this and they are always searching for a better way to do things. The successful person does not ask 'Can I do it better?'. He knows he can! She knows she can!

While *everyone* possesses innate creative potential, it is more pronounced in some people than in others. However, it is most certainly a skill that can be developed more fully.

There are many methods of tapping the creative mind, just as there is no one way to decorate a house, landscape a lawn, make a sale, rear a child, or cook a steak. In other words, there are as many best ways as there are creative minds. The following methods can be used to stimulate and develop your ideas.

23 WAYS TO GENERATE IDEAS

1. WHAT IF ...?

What if it were larger? Or smaller? *What if* it were turned upside down? Inside out? *What if* it were made from a different kind of material? Cheaper material? *What if* it were thinner, lighter, shorter? *What if* it were a different colour?

General economic decline and depopulation of many rural areas has led to the closing down or relocation of several industries. When a rural-based chicken farm closed down, a local resident identified the potential for a lucrative business and established an economically viable, small-scale chicken farm to meet the local community's needs.

Exploring 'What if ...?' questions often helps you uncover new ideas and resources. *What if* certain goods that we take for granted were unavailable? *What if* a supplier were unable to meet a retailer's order? *What if* the specific product were sold at a cheaper price? Retailers are dependent on manufacturers and suppliers for stock. Should production of an 'essential item' be halted for some reason, this could create a market gap and a business opportunity for the enterprising entrepreneur.

2. TURN PROBLEMS INTO PROFITS

Often, something that appears to be a problem (*see* box) is overlooked as a source of potential profit.

The task of clearing land that was overrun by a hardy, bush-like shrub proved extremely labour intensive, and motivated a farmer to reassess the 'problem'. On inspection, it was discovered that the wood was perfect for making charcoal and was particularly popular for its aromatic properties. Supplying the local market became a viable business opportunity.

Keep in mind that the first solution to a problem may not always be the best solution. Many businesses have grown out of what was at first regarded as a problem and generate lucrative income.

3. VISUALIZE

Business successes, engineering triumphs and medical breakthroughs were all *visualized* before they became realities. Everything, from satellites to skyscrapers to baby food, is an idea that was acted upon.

Visualization is a technique which brings to the fore ideas and/or perceptions which are often unrealized in the routines of every-day-life. Through visualization, a mental picture of a product or service can be created. Often, these mental images are summarily dismissed as they appear unattainable. Some people, however, develop their creative visualizations into businesses.

A gym instructor noticed that many of the women who attended her class wore ill-fitting leotards. She visualized what they would look like in custom-made garments and this led her to consider the prospect of starting a side-line business producing activewear. She put together a few of her designs and began wearing them to the gym. The compliments flowed and she now offers a range of made-to-order activewear.

4. EXPRESS YOUR CREATIVITY

Make a list of what you enjoy doing and do better than most people. Are you a great cook? Are you a genius at fixing things around the house? Are you a whiz at mathematics? Do people admire your garden?

If you have a particular skill or hobby, you could turn it into an income-producing business. In this age of plasticized, homogenized everything, craftspeople and cottage-industry entrepreneurs are finding a new, appreciative market *and* making money from it.

Can you sell the finished product? Could your interest be offered as a service to others? Could you teach your skills to someone else?

5. IDENTIFY NEEDS

What do people *need?* The basics include food, clothing, housing and education, but there is also the ever-present demand for entertainment, travel, status and other psychological needs.

Needs can be identified by reading articles in newspapers, magazines and journals. Make a list of apparent needs and then think of ways in which these needs can be met. You may come up with a great idea that will fill a gap in the market.

The following list identifies several needs and ways in which they can be met. These ideas are aimed at providing essential services for the community, as well as creating job opportunities.

Food	advising on farming skills; bottling preserves; restaurant; home delivery service
Clothing	teaching sewing/mending; selling second-hand clothes
Housing	making bricks; teaching building skills; transporting materials; hiring machinery; fixing up old houses and reselling them; furniture removal
Child care	day-mother; crèche/playgroup; youth/community centre

6. FORCED CONNECTIONS

Many products and services have been developed through lateral thinking and forcing connections between two seemingly unrelated concepts – examples include the clock-radio and the wrist watch. Scan your surroundings and force a connection between two seemingly unrelated things. Don't worry if the connection is obscure – it may just spark off an idea for a new business venture!

Consider the forced connection between shops and maps. A business opportunity arising from this could be the production of an illustrated city map that promotes small business. Other maps could be designed to focus on entertainment facilities or restaurants in a particular area.

7. KEEP A RECORD OF YOUR IDEAS

Every day many good ideas are forgotten because they are not recorded. Carry a notebook and, when you get an idea, write it down in as much detail as possible.

Keep a 'creativity success' file in which all the ideas that you have written down can be filed. Examine your storehouse of ideas on a regular basis. At first, an idea may have no apparent value, but if it has any promise, keep it!

Articles and advertisements in magazines and newspapers often act as catalysts in suggesting business opportunities.

8. BE RECEPTIVE TO IDEAS

How would you react if someone told you that they intended making money recycling rubbish, or turning old bottles into unique wineglasses, making a living selling surplus products, or making furniture from plastic? Your reaction could very well be: 'It won't work', 'The economy is bad', 'It's a stupid idea' or 'Where are you going to get the money from to do it?' It is important *not* to discard ideas that appear silly or impractical at the outset – many have, in fact, been turned into very successful businesses.

9. READ WIDELY AND ACTIVELY

Every newspaper and magazine is crammed with information that may give rise to an idea for a business opportunity. Advertisements can also trigger ideas for new products and services.

Newspapers and magazines also report on things that people are interested in and concerned about; you may pick up some market demands from these and discover a way to satisfy them.

Consider the products and services that could be identified from the following extract:

Ready for roles beyond school
Schools cannot cure the world's economic ills, but they can be a fertile ground for the later creation of wealth by preparing children for the realities of the workplace.
(The Star, 28 February 1994)

What can be done to meet the needs of an exacting and demanding workplace? Which skills and what form of entrepreneurial training could be provided? Here are some ideas:

- *Run seminars and workshops on how to develop entrepreneurial skills.*
- *Write/publish self-study manuals on business ideas and the prospects of self-employment.*
- *Offer audio-visual material to assist vocational guidance in schools.*

10. CULTIVATE YOUR IDEAS

Combine your initial idea with related ideas. You can achieve this by attending seminars, workshops or courses, and collecting and reading material on the subject/s you are interested in. Think of potential uses for a particular product.

11. TRY SOMETHING NEW

Break fixed routines and expose yourself to new interests. Do something you wouldn't normally do.

Often the 'new' will interconnect with the 'old' in novel and potentially fascinating ways. Some of the positive side-effects of this type of planned self-development include increased self-worth and stimulated creativity, which acts as a catalyst for generating ideas.

12. BE PROGRESSIVE, NOT REGRESSIVE

Replace 'That's the way it's always been done' with 'Can it be done better?'. The idea is not to reject existing concepts, but to re-evaluate them and find ways of expanding and improving on them. Ask the question, 'What could be used instead of this product or service?'

13. BRAINSTORMING

Brainstorming is a popular group creativity technique. Each participant is briefed on the subject to be 'brainstormed', and a recorder is nominated to write down the ideas as they arise (including the seemingly 'wild' ones). The aim is to generate as many ideas as possible.

It is important that the entire group contribute to the idea-generating process and remain focused on the issue at hand. Emphasis in the initial stage is on the quantity, rather than quality of ideas developed. Participants should not criticize, evaluate or comment on any of the ideas raised at this stage as it could inhibit some member's participation. The second phase of brainstorming involves evaluating the ideas.

14. IMPROVE ON EXISTING IDEAS

Browse around shops, trade shows, fairs, flea markets and exhibitions and consider ideas which may improve existing products or services. How can a particular product or service be adapted or modified for a new use?

For example, a range of hand-made children's clothes may attract your attention at a fair, but you may have several creative ideas on how to improve on the product – for example, adding colourful appliqués or a smocked yoke.

Another way of using an existing idea is to investigate businesses that have gone bankrupt. In many cases the opportunity to develop the idea has remained sound even though the organization went bankrupt.

There may be many reasons for their bankruptcy. For instance, the idea was ahead of its time, the market was correctly identified but poorly utilized or the idea has great potential but the financial management was poor. Another reason for bankruptcy may actually be the result of the product or service's success: the business may not have had the resources 'to ride out' the product and market development costs; consequently, cash-flow problems created by expansion could not be solved.

A list of these businesses is published in local and national newspapers, and your local Chamber of Commerce can provide you with relevant information.

15. BRAINWRITING

Brainwriting, a non-verbal method of developing ideas, is similar to brainstorming. This method can be used with a group of any size. Each participant is briefed on the subject under consideration or the issue to be resolved.

Participants are instructed to write down four ideas or comments that address the issue. The papers are then placed in the centre of the table, shuffled, and each person draws a piece of paper that has been written on by someone else.

At this point, everyone will have a piece of paper with four ideas written on it. The participants write down four more ideas, either original or 'piggy-backed', based on those already written on the page. This process continues until the participants run out of ideas. A single list of ideas can then be compiled and evaluated, and these may generate even more new ideas.

16. SERENDIPITY TECHNIQUE

This technique is based on the production of ideas 'by chance'. The purpose of the serendipity technique is to stimulate the creative mind by allowing it to see things 'differently' and, in effect, allows new ideas to be generated.

For example, cut-up images taken from magazines and newspapers can be arranged in any form that comes to mind. This exercise cannot be expected to generate a concrete idea for a business, but is meant to develop patterns and associations to stimulate thinking.

17. CREATIVE UNHAPPINESS

Paying attention to your own and others' complaints about existing products or services may lead you to new and exciting ideas.

Take note of the things that irritate you: long lines at the supermarket, a gadget that won't work properly, incompetent salespeople, surly waiters, cleaning up after the dog, unsynchronized traffic lights ...

Remember that things that annoy you will tend to bother other people too. If you can find a way of reducing or getting rid of some petty annoyance, people will be glad to pay you for your solution.

For example, a paraplegic found that narrow aeroplane aisles and inaccessible hotels dampened his enthusiasm for travelling. Turning this frustration into a business opportunity, he developed a collapsible wheelchair.

18. MIND MAPPING

Mind mapping is another technique that stimulates creativity. It is closely related to the forced connections technique in that both rely on lateral, non-linear thinking.

The central idea is written in the centre of a large sheet of paper. Radiating lines lead to various related ideas, queries or conclusions.

Its purpose is to create a simple framework of thoughts. Further research generates more factual material and allow you to validate or reject any information. Associated points and concepts can then be linked with lines, shading or highlighting pens.

You will be surprised at how many thoughts can be triggered by these patterns – new concepts, new perspectives, new associations of ideas. Once you have sketched your 'map', display it where you can see it regularly.

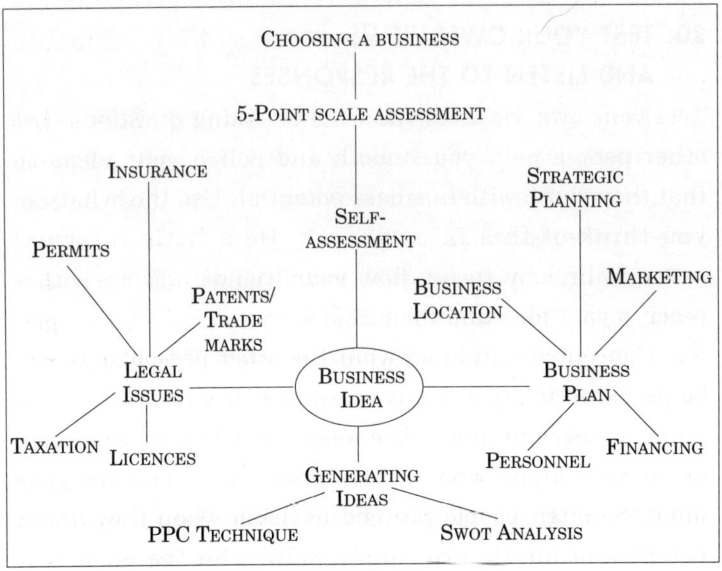

19. LISTEN!

Listening to people's opinions on different matters can unlock your creativity. This will get you thinking in new ways because the diversity of their opinions can unlock your own creativity and help to make up your mind about an idea for a business.

In personal conversations or in group meetings, encourage people to talk to you in the following ways, 'Tell me about your experience ...', 'Why do you think this happens ...?', 'What is the purpose of ...?' or, 'What do you think should be done about ...?' or, 'What do you think is the key point?' There are several creative benefits to stimulating others to talk: their conversation may suggest new ideas or concepts which can be used as business opportunities, confirm existing ideas which you need feedback on, or remind you of things you may have forgotten.

20. TEST YOUR OWN VIEWS AND LISTEN TO THE RESPONSES

Test your own views in the form of asking questions. Let other people help you smooth and polish your ideas so that they shine with business potential. Use the 'what-do-you-think-of-this ...' approach. Do a little informal research first by seeing how your friends and associates react to your idea and then ...

... Concentrate fully on what the other person says and be prepared to answer any questions they may have. Listening is more than just keeping quiet when someone else is talking; allow what is being said to penetrate your mind. So often people pretend to listen when they aren't listening at all; they're simply waiting for the other person to pause so that they can take over. For instance, you might be planning to manufacture a portable, briefcase-sized barbecue grill. The one aspect you are still deliberating over is whether it should be wood-burning or charcoal. Your discussions with outsiders about the concept may lead to feedback that is not all positive; however, concentrate on what the other person says, and evaluate it objectively and realistically without becoming defensive about retaining your original thoughts about the idea. It is only by doing this that you will be able to reap the benefits of their opinions.

21. SHARPEN YOUR BRAIN

Learn to play strategy games like chess, backgammon or bridge. Learn a foreign language – something that is useful as well as stimulating. Force your brain to think in new patterns. Do jigsaw and crossword puzzles.

The purpose of pursuing these exercises is to stimulate creative and developmental thinking processes. In other words, they make you aware of options, choices and obstacles, and expand the boundaries of your personal horizon. The effect is one of enhancing your ability to make future decisions and choices (which is essential to business success), as well as making you more perceptive to the possibilities surrounding you.

22. JOIN COMMUNITY ORGANIZATIONS

Become a member of the local Chamber of Commerce. As a member, you will attend all their meetings, participate in Chamber affairs and become acquainted with prominent business people. You may want to join other local clubs and organizations to broaden your perspective and knowledge of a certain subject, for example, photography or art.

By working alongside and communicating with people that have the same interests, you are exposed to first-hand information about market trends, trade decisions, and the generation of new ideas.

Other advantages include learning the ropes from senior members, and being able to consult with them about the pros and cons of developing your ideas into a viable, profit-making business.

23. BECOME A COLLECTOR OF VISUAL IMAGES

Try pinning interest-related pictures, articles or notes on a wall-chart or pinboard in a place you see regularly. For instance, if your interest lies in promoting pre-school education, the type of article and information you will collect will probably comprise advertisements for encyclopaedias, an article on the secrets of studying, a pamphlet advertising character glove puppets, a note from a playgroup in your suburb looking for voluntary assistants, and newspaper cuttings depicting the dire need for better education programmes.

Seeing the related information in a collective context, will result in a 'trigger effect' (one idea setting off another) which will help your mind to source and incubate new ideas. This may, for example, inspire you to write an easy-to-read booklet aimed at parents of pre-school children on 'How to prepare your child for formal schooling'. Your single-minded approach in this respect will lead you to collect even more visual images as you begin to generate ideas in writing the booklet, focusing on aspects such as skills, listening, colours, language, reading, textures, position and direction. Such a booklet would promote school-readiness by encouraging youngsters to question and think for themselves, and this, in turn, helps build self-confidence.

CHAPTER

2

ASSESSING AND DEVELOPING YOUR IDEAS

■

CASIE

PPC TECHNIQUE

SWOT ANALYSIS

CHOOSING AN IDEA

ASSESSING THE MARKET FOR YOUR IDEA

PROTECTING YOUR IDEA

■

To assess whether the idea (or ideas) generated has the potential to become a real business opportunity, the essential aspects of the idea need to be evaluated. The more you know about your idea, the easier it will be to make the decision to proceed or not.

CASIE

The following exercise, CASIE, offers guidelines to help you organize your thoughts, evaluate problems, and make decisions about your ideas:

Collect information on the specific subject: view films, television and video programmes; attend lectures, courses, seminars, workshops; gather written material that might help you gain further knowledge and take notes for future reference.

Analyse and arrange this information. Take your time when considering an idea's viability, and develop it to the stage where it is an opportunity obviously worth pursuing.

Select what is relevant. You will need a clear outline of when, where and how to apply the new information.

Implement your decision. Once you have a clearly defined plan of action to turn your idea into a business, you will find it easier to carry out.

Evaluate the results of the CASIE exercise and establish whether you need more information.

There are several ways of assessing whether an idea can then be turned into a viable business opportunity. The PPC technique and the SWOT analysis are both aimed at evaluating basic concepts and providing feedback.

PPC TECHNIQUE

Write the idea at the top of a sheet of paper and divide the page into three sections. Head the sections: positive, possibilities, concerns, and evaluate your idea according to these three points.

Positive: What do you like about the idea?
Possibilities: Itemize possible applications or extensions of the idea.
Concerns: Document your concerns about the proposal.

THE PPC TECHNIQUE IN PRACTICE

Idea: A mail-order business

Positive

- *Low investment if articles manufactured by self, only 'made to order', or bought on consignment (manufacturer is paid when you receive payment)*
- *Business can be started on a part-time basis, at home.*
- *Profit-making opportunities.*

Possibilities

- *Specialize in selected articles or offer a wide range of goods.*
- *Expansion by employing agents countrywide.*
- *International markets.*

Concerns

- *Difficulty in locating suitable products.*
- *Ability to meet large orders.*
- *Hiring people to help with orders, packaging and postage.*
- *Collecting payment from clients.*
- *Dealing with returned goods.*
- *Premises too small to accommodate stock.*

SWOT ANALYSIS

Write the idea at the top of a sheet of paper and draw four vertical columns on the page. Head the columns: strengths, weaknesses, opportunities, threats. Evaluate your idea according to these four points.

Strengths:	List all the positive aspects of the idea.
Weaknesses:	Identify the areas which may be problematic and evaluate whether these problems can be overcome.
Opportunities:	What opportunities can be created or identified?
Threats:	Consider reasons why the idea may fail.

CHOOSING AN IDEA

By now, it should be apparent that a good idea, or what appears to be a good idea, is not enough on its own to support a business. The prospective entrepreneur who wants to put his or her ideas to work must possess or develop the ability and perseverance to see ideas through to fruition.

It is important also to eliminate those ideas and options that are incompatible with personal likes and dislikes and those that will not provide the challenges, opportunities and financial rewards that you seek. Be prepared to spend time researching your ideas' business potential. It may be beneficial to draft a preliminary business plan for each idea.

Entrepreneurs are dependent on feedback, and one of the best ways to put your ideas to the test is to conduct some informal market research. Brainstorm your ideas with a group of friends or family members, and find out what they think. Ask them which of the products or services they find appealing. Talk to people who are already linked to the specific industry or trade. This will help to confirm what you already know about the business and may provide you with new information on which to base a decision.

Alternatively, you could start your business on a mini scale, even if this means manufacturing one prototype of each article you plan to produce on a large scale.

You will have to determine whether the product or service has sales appeal – the product must have something that inspires customers to buy it. But there is a second type of sales appeal that is just as important: your merchandise will only have sales appeal *for you* if it shows a reasonable profit. Test the marketability of your product or service by analyzing reactions from those who see or experience it. If your business idea is service-related (for example, photography or typing) equip yourself with the necessary tools and approach prospective clients with the offer of completing an assignment for them, free of charge. *Ask* for feedback. Take cognisance of any comments, criticisms, preferences and suggestions, and make adaptations or changes where necessary. If the response to your first mini market-survey is encouraging, it's time to seriously consider your idea as a business opportunity.

ASSESSING THE MARKET FOR YOUR IDEA

The base of success in any business is the existence of a real opportunity: there must be customers in the marketplace who want to buy the goods or services being offered.

There are two ways of identifying business opportunities. The first is to start with the belief that the marketplace can always accommodate a good product sold at a low price. The advantage of this concept is twofold: the introduction of new products not only stimulates product competition, but also aims at satisfying consumer demand for new and budget-priced products. While this combination of 'good product' and 'low price' may appeal to some customers, many may reject one or the other. Low price does not necessarily ensure success. Offering your product or service at a low price does not necessarily ensure success. In fact, a low price is self-defeating if people assume that low price means low quality.

Low price is a good strategy when the market is highly competitive, people know the benefits of the product or service, and there is little difference between one company's product/service and another's.

Given this situation, the entrepreneur is faced with the challenge to prove to potential customers that the product or service offered is equal to or better than one that is currently available.

The second approach to determining whether an idea has business opportunity potential is to use a marketing orientation strategy.

Essentially, the direction the proposed business will take should be clearly understood. The potential small business owner will need to answer questions like, 'What product or service will the customer buy?', 'Is there a market for the product?' and, if so, 'How big is the market?' Answers to these questions can be obtained by conducting specific market research.

CONDUCT A FACT-FINDING STUDY

By conducting a fact-finding study, you should be able to identify your target market (prospective customers), where they live, how they think, why they will buy the product or service from you, and what they will be prepared to pay for it. You should also be able to identify any competition, either current or potential, assess their prices and, in the case of an operating business, why customers choose to buy there.

The most effective way of gathering this information is through personal or telephone interviews and questionnaires/surveys.

Questionnaires

This method of information research is often time-consuming, but will provide valuable and accurate information on which sound decisions can be made. Questionnaires can either be dropped in postboxes for people to fill in, in their own time, or used as the basis for a research interview.

The questions asked should enable you to identify the composition of your market according to, for example, gender, age, education, occupation, income level and other characteristics that may affect the demand for your goods and/or services.

In compiling a questionnaire it is important to address the issue of bias – the way in which a question is phrased can lead to a particular (sometimes biased) response.

For example, if the owner of a rug-cleaning company asks, 'Would you consider using my company to clean your rugs?', the respondent will probably answer 'Yes'.

The respondent is not saying that he or she *will* use the company – only that he or she will *consider* it. If, however, the question had been 'How do you clean your rugs?', the answers would indicate how many people hire professional companies and how many do it themselves. The next question could be, 'Why do you hire a professional company?' or, 'Why do you do the job yourself?' Answers may indicate objections to the cost of hiring a professional cleaning service or that the service is not available over weekends or after-hours. The reasons you are given may generate new ideas which can be explored and used to expand your business.

The information gathered from questionnaires can then be analyzed. Continuing with the above example, the percentage of respondents who hire a professional rug cleaning services can be calculated. Then you must consider how many homes will use this service every year? How many firms offer a similar (competitive) service? What percentage of this market can your company capture? By answering these questions, you may conclude that it is better to establish your business in another geographic area or that most of your business could be derived from an after-hours/weekend service.

Various associations, direct mail marketing groups, companies who mail monthly accounts to customers, schools, clubs, and so forth, could be approached to mail your questionnaire along with their regular correspondence for a small fee. Be sure to ask the respondent to include his or her name, address and/or telephone number on the returned questionnaire. In this way, you can build up your own qualified list of potential customers.

Interviews

Prepared questions are often used as the basis for a personal research interview. An in-store interview to determine customers' reactions to different types of products can be most effective and retailers, in particular, tend to use this approach with ease.

Interviews can also be conducted over the telephone, but a survey based on random telephone number selection is not cost-effective and should be used only as a last resort.

When interviewing over the telephone, take the opportunity of expanding your list of names and telephone numbers by asking the interviewee for referrals.

INTERPRETING RESULTS

If your questions were specific, the results should show who will buy, why they will buy, and where they will buy, what they are prepared to pay, and indicate the size of the market.

The results should identify possible weaknesses in your product or service, challenge assumptions and critically examine the business' 'flop' potential. Factors affecting your market, such as expendable income and the location of your business, can also be identified.

The results should allow you to gauge the general outlook for your particular business, as well as the product's potential to attract a larger portion of the market.

On the downside, the results may show that there is not a sufficiently large niche in the market to accommodate your product or service. The next critical question is, 'What will differentiate your product or service from the rest?' What is your competitive advantage?

IMPLEMENTING IDEAS

So, you have now assessed the business potential of your idea by interpreting the results of your fact-finding study. Feedback should also enable you to develop the concept of your business more fully. With all this information taken into consideration, you can now decide whether you want to go ahead and implement your idea/s for a business or not.

PROTECTING YOUR IDEA

An idea for a 'unique' design, trade secret, method, product or device must be thoroughly developed before it is patented. Design protection will then be granted for the shape or configuration of a new article, such as a car or a teacup, or the pattern of a new design, for example, for use on fabric or wallpaper.

The Patents Act in South Africa allows for a 12-month period of development by granting what is known as a 'provisional patent'. In other words, you are required to develop, manufacture, market and distribute your product within 12 months of the date of registration. During this time, no-one else can take out a patent on your idea.

If you intend exporting or earning royalties in foreign countries, you will need to protect yourself abroad. To obtain a full patent you will have to employ a patent attorney to 'search' through the patent registers in each country in which you want your patent to be safeguarded.

You may need the confirmation of experts to assist you before your idea finally crystallizes into a patent-worthy device, method or process which can be registered. This could be very costly and you need to budget for it carefully before entering into any research or design agreements. A full South African patent is valid for 20 years. You may also consider registering a design or trademark. A registered design is valid for five years and does not give you the same protection as a patent; a competitor is at liberty to use the same principles and ideas providing they are not identical in every aspect.

A trademark is a means of identifying certain goods and services. It is a symbol used to distinguish your product or service from those of others, and should be aimed at your target market. The trademark may be, among other things, a device, label, name, signature, word/s, numerals or any combination of these. The registration of a trademark lasts indefinitely, providing you continue to renew it.

If your idea involves written work (this specifically applies to authors, artists, playwrights and composers), you simply write your name, the word 'copyright' (or use the symbol ©) and the date on the work you want to protect. For example:

Brian Smith © October 1993

This procedure will ensure the protection of your work for your entire lifetime and an additional 15 years thereafter.

James Smith © October 1998

CHAPTER

3

SELF ASSESSMENT TO STARTING-UP

■

ENTREPRENEURIAL TRAITS

SELF-ASSESSMENT ANALYSIS

GOING IT ALONE

RISKS AND REWARDS

WHERE WILL YOU WORK?

■

The entrepreneurial mentality was once the exception to the rule: during the industrial era, most people flocked to be employees. In the post-industrial era the best and brightest workers were still trained to work for large institutions. In the future, however, the entrepreneurial section of the economy is going to be taken up by a far greater percentage of the population. Futurists predict that at the turn of the century, 50% of our population will comprise entrepreneurs. Some will be true, driven entrepreneurs; others will be forced to *learn* how to become entrepreneurs. An individual's traits, skills and capabilities usually match his/her entrepreneurial preference (type of business). Before proceeding with the self-assessment analysis section, it's useful to look at the different types of entrepreneur and their traits.

OPPORTUNISTIC ENTREPRENEUR

An opportunistic entrepreneur focuses on continual change and the creation of new conditions and enterprises in order to seize any opportunities which present themselves. This type of entrepreneur maintains constant contact with sources who have access to information about people's needs; focuses on the medium- and long-term rather than the short-term; is confident of his or her ability to interact with others; and the decisions he or she makes usually have far-reaching implications.

INVENTREPRENEUR

The inventrepreneur is motivated by mental enrichment and reward associated with innovations. He or she sees the enterprise as an instrument of discovery and innovation – the actual growth of the enterprise is not of primary concern. There are two types of inventrepreneur. The one can be found in businesses where the main objective is to invent or create something new, irrespective of external influences such as economic trends or market demand. The other type of inventrepreneur is specifically consumer-oriented, and is found in businesses that work within the parameters of adapting conditions and given market restrictions.

CRAFTSPERSON/TECHNICAL ENTREPRENEUR

The technical entrepreneur is interested primarily in the innovative uses of existing production technology. He or she is a craftsperson, preferring to be involved with the product or the production process rather than with other workers. Generally, the craftsperson's orientation is short-term rather than long-term.

PIONEERING ENTREPRENEUR

The pioneering entrepreneur, by definition, is prepared to be the first to test an invention or an idea in the business environment. This type of entrepreneur can be found taking the lead in his or her particular industry and is a risk-taker *par excellence*.

COPYCAT ENTREPRENEUR

This type of entrepreneur engages in business activities only *after* the invention or idea has been successfully launched in the business environment. The copycat entrepreneur may not be sufficiently confident, or have too little time or money, to be a 'pioneer'.

ENTREPRENEURIAL TRAITS

Motivated by an inner compulsion to achieve, the 'typical' entrepreneur is undeterred by difficulties and set-backs, is willing to take risks, is decisive, versatile, self-confident and task-oriented. It is incorrect to assume, however, that *all* entrepreneurs possess these characteristics from the outset. In fact, many prospective business owners may not have the inclination to seek total control or enjoy taking risks, or may fear losing self-confidence in the face of adversity. With increased confidence, knowledge and experience, however, it is possible to develop several traits.

TOTAL DEDICATION, DETERMINATION AND PERSEVERANCE

These are probably the most important characteristics that contribute to entrepreneurial success. They equip the entrepreneur with the inner strength necessary to ensure survival in today's fiercely competitive business environment.

DRIVE TO ACHIEVE AND TO GROW

Successful entrepreneurs want to excel at their endeavours and often surpass their own expectations. While profitable performance is an objective, measurable criterion, it isn't the *only* goal pursued by the entrepreneur – growth and achievement are just as important.

Entrepreneurs gain personal satisfaction from creating and developing an enterprise. They are motivated by the desire to achieve, rather than by an obsession with status and power.

ABILITY TO FOCUS ON OPPORTUNITIES AND GOALS

Entrepreneurs concentrate their efforts on identifying new opportunities and goals, and then determining how these can be backed up or supported by resources, structures and strategies.

TAKING INITIATIVE AND PERSONAL RESPONSIBILITY

Entrepreneurs are regarded as key figures in a free-market economy. They prefer situations in which they are held personally responsible – regardless of whether the end result is a success or a failure. They are independent and it is not necessary for them to meet standards set by others. True entrepreneurs prefer to lead, and use their initiative in solving problems.

Successful entrepreneurs have ample self-confidence. This goes hand-in-hand with their motivation to achieve and their desire to accept personal responsibility.

PROBLEM SOLVING

Entrepreneurs view difficult circumstances as challenges; however, they are aware of their own limitations and seek professional advice when necessary.

OPTIMISTIC REALISM AND A SENSE OF HUMOUR

Entrepreneurs acknowledge their strengths and weaknesses, and harbour no illusions about their abilities. These individuals are optimistic and realistic. In most cases, their realism is complemented by a healthy sense of humour which is necessary to keep things in perspective and identify the positive aspects of an unfavourable set of events.

SEEKING AND USING FEEDBACK

Growth-oriented entrepreneurs are dependent on regular feedback, both positive and negative, for two reasons: to keep track of how well they are doing with their business, and to guide them in improving their performance. This trait helps entrepreneurs to learn from any mistakes they make, and encourages them to be careful listeners and quick learners.

CALCULATING RISKS AND RISK DISTRIBUTION

While successful entrepreneurs are not essentially gamblers, they are prepared to take risks. Apart from risking money, they also risk their reputation when they pursue a new business venture. They try to eliminate any unnecessary risks and tend to take fewer risks once they have proved and established themselves. Nevertheless, accepting the elements of risk is an inextricable part of the quest for profit – often the greater the risk, the greater the profit.

INTEGRITY AND TRUSTWORTHINESS

These are two essential qualities which are necessary for any and all successful, long-term personal and business relationships. An entrepreneur who lacks these characteristics is heading for failure.

RESOLUTENESS, URGENCY AND PATIENCE

The successful entrepreneur has clear vision and plans ahead, while putting every effort into the project at hand at any particular time. Patience plays a vital role in every successful business.

ABILITY TO DEAL WITH THE FEAR OF FAILURE

The threat of failure is ever-present in small business, and it is therefore essential that the entrepreneur be well-versed in all aspects of running a business.

If there is a chance that the business venture will lead to failure, the true entrepreneur will deal with the possibility by re-evaluating his or her business, so that any concerns and weaknesses can be identified, dealt with and eliminated and/or alternative plans put into action.

By contrast, people who are afraid of failure usually concentrate on risk-free activities, negating any motivation they may have to be successful.

TEAM BUILDER AND CREATOR OF ACHIEVERS

People who create and develop successful businesses usually do not work in isolation. They are not interested in taking all the credit for themselves because they know that it is seldom possible to build a significant enterprise single-handed. They proactively build a team of workers, and reward them with responsibilities, and share the credit for any achievements.

ABILITY TO MOTIVATE SELF AND OTHERS

Entrepreneurs have a strong desire to succeed and are driven by an 'inner force' which inevitably affects those who work with them. Their positive attitude and optimism is contagious, and manifests itself in many ways – for example, high productivity, staff loyalty and co-operation, encourage in-house communication and good customer relations.

TENACITY

Successful entrepreneurs are purposeful and tenacious in their endeavours. They keep a close watch on developments, and can alter their course, if necessary, to progress and gain good results.

ABILITY TO COMMUNICATE/NEGOTIATE

The successful entrepreneur has the ability to relate to and deal with all kinds of personalities. It is the entrepreneur's responsibility to share relevant information with his employees, suppliers and customers.

HEALTHY SELF-ESTEEM

It is vital that all entrepreneurs have good opinions of themselves. Lack of self-confidence can affect the entrepreneur's credibility in the eyes of employees and customers alike, as well as the profitability of the business. A positive self-image is often synonymous with a successful business, quality service and reliable goods, and vice versa.

However, an entrepreneur's confidence may take a knock when a serious problem arises. For instance, he or she may be concerned about financing, delivery problems, lack of resources, or debts. Finding a way to solve those problems will restore confidence.

SELF-ASSESSMENT ANALYSIS

The purpose of completing a self-assessment analysis is to identify the range of abilities you have at your disposal. You need to assess your attitude towards a specific activity, your health and stamina, and analyse/evaluate your personal objectives, interests, economic status and responsibilities. These criteria must be considered in determining whether you have the necessary expertise and inclination to run your own business.

1. My objectives in life include: | ***Yes*** | ***No***

- *Making a great deal of money*
- *Being my own boss*
- *Living comfortably*
- *Working for someone else*
- *Providing employment for others*
- *Providing products / services*
- *Investing whatever time and effort is necessary to achieve success*
- *Experiencing self-fulfilment in my work*

2. Education:

- *Primary school* ____________________
- *High school* ____________________
- *Technical school* ____________________
- *College* ____________________
  Number of years ____________________
  Diploma / Certificate ____________________
  Major subject(s) ____________________
  Other ____________________
- *University* ____________________
  Number of years ____________________
  Degree ____________________
  Major subject(s) ____________________
  Master's degree ____________________
  Field(s) ____________________
  Other ____________________

3. Work experience:

- *Current / last occupation* ____________________
  Employer ____________________
  Skills gained ____________________

➥

- *Occupation* ______
  Employer ______
  Skills gained ______
- *Occupation* ______
  Employer ______
  Skills gained ______
- *Occupation* ______
  Employer ______
  Skills gained ______

5. *My skills/talents are:* ______

6. *How do I display creativity? (e.g. hobby)* ______

7. *Where have my creative ideas been put to practical use? (e.g. organized projects, design presentations)* ______

8. *My abilities include:*

	Yes	**No**
■ *Directing the activities of others*		
■ *Planning and organizing an activity in a manner that takes the least time, effort and material*		
■ *Serving people in a pleasing manner*		
■ *Helping people resolve their personal differences*		
■ *Managing money*		
■ *Keeping records*		
■ *Being my own boss/self-starter*		
■ *Taking initiative and personal responsibility*		
■ *Making decisions*		
■ *Generating new ideas for products and services*		
■ *Problem-solving*		
■ *Dealing with stress*		

Once you have completed the self-assessment analysis, compare your capabilities and characteristics with the entrepreneurial traits discussed earlier. Do you have what it takes? Review those areas that require further training and/or development and work out a plan to 'fill-in the gaps'. Consider the options of further study. One method is self-study – either by enrolling for a course with a correspondence college or reading a selection of books which have been published on business-related topics. Or you may choose to develop your abilities through organized courses. These are offered on a semi-formal basis by various institutions, and includes lecture demonstrations, workshops and seminars. Formal degree and/or diploma courses are offered at universities and technikons, and through correspondence colleges.

GOING IT ALONE

For a variety of reasons, many people aspire to self-employment. These include wanting to earn more money, gain a sense of independence, meaning, identity, creativity and achievement.

Planning is essential before starting any business and you should be aware of the many advantages and disadvantages of self-employment. Your personal goals and specific financial needs will have to be evaluated and you must assess whether self-employment will help you to attain these goals.

Many people approach business ownership with a degree of caution and first 'test the water' of entrepreneurship, either by starting an independent micro small-businesses on a part-time basis, or by moonlighting or freelancing to earn extra money. Others enter the arena of the self-employed more daringly by risking everything to make a success of the business. However, for many people in South Africa, starting an independent business is not merely a challenge, but rather the only way of surviving in the face of unemployment.

Prospective entrepreneurs include the physically disabled and retired people who are looking for a way to supplement their pension. Unemployed school-leavers and those who are unhappy with their present work situation, may also turn to self-employment. Those people finding themselves in this situation, need to evaluate their talents and find ways of turning their job experience, skills and hobbies into paying propositions. Others will be motivated to earn larger incomes to finance and enjoy expensive lifestyles.

There is also a rapidly growing number of home-based entrepreneurs who are able to fulfil their domestic commitments while taking on part-time or freelance work responsibilities.

Regardless of the reason or motivation, one of the first things you should do if you are considering starting a small business is to decide whether running a business is the right thing for you to pursue. To make this decision, you will have to define your current work and financial situation and compare this with what you expect to achieve through self-employment.

JOB CONTENT

Most employees are less concerned with the traditional rewards – raises and promotions – for work done, and are more adamant about their needs for a positive work environment, flexibility and time to devote to their personal lives. Consequently, the job satisfaction criteria have changed considerably over the years. Before accepting or leaving a job, many employees will question the possible effect/s on their personal and family lives. In recent times, fewer people are willing to sacrifice their quality of life to get ahead.

WORKING HOURS

Many employees seek options such as flexitime, part-time work, working from home, job sharing – anything that allows them the flexibility to take care of their personal responsibilities and aspirations.

Some employees, however, find that they are confined to a working day that is routine and unstimulating, and decide that their time could be put to more productive use on their own projects.

Understaffing is another aspect which may influence working hours. In attempting to meet excess workloads, staff very often become stressed and ultimately unproductive. Ineffective time management may also compel employees to work after-hours. This contributes to resignations as individual employees often feel that their time can be utilized more effectively and productively in their own, individual businesses.

Running a business often means spending long hours working on financial accounts, sales plans, marketing and promotional ideas and general administration. It also means sacrificing weekends, holidays, and family time. The entrepreneur-in-the-making does not have the same resources at his or her disposal as larger companies, and he or she has to play the role of bookkeeper, salesperson, marketing manager and general manager rolled into one.

It is important to guard against becoming an obsessive 'workaholic', which will place additional strain on your family, relationships and your health. Entertaining clients often takes place after-hours, and some people will have to consider whether their personal commitments will restrict this type of activity.

Vendors, hawkers, craftspeople and artisans may choose to operate their particular businesses on a part-time basis. However, circumstances may at times demand that they work long hours to meet a deadline for an urgent or large order.

WORKING WITH PEOPLE

Some people are natural communicators and are able to find common ground with most of the people they meet. However, it is unreasonable to expect every individual to be like the inconstant chameleon, and to be versatile in every aspect of sustaining good communication. You are entitled to have a difference of opinion, but it is important that you maintain your dignity and professionalism. In assessing your situation, you will have to consider whether you prefer working independently or in association with other people.

CONSULTANTS

Take into consideration that you may need to consult with lawyers, accountants, patent attorneys, tax advisers, insurance agents or brokers, and business consultants, depending on your particular requirements. Remember that these consultations will add to the costs of setting up your idea as a business.

RISKS AND REWARDS

It's tough enough manoeuvring a business in a stable economy, but it's even tougher in a rollercoaster economy beset with bankruptcies. In a fiercely competitive business environment, survival depends on anticipating the unexpected. It is very important to be aware of the risks involved in owning and running a small business.

Smaller businesses are particularly vulnerable to bankruptcy and failure, especially if they are dependent upon a few large customers, and if their customers are concentrated in a small number of volatile industries or a few geographic locations. Companies in seasonal industries also face high risks. For example, a manufacturing firm that makes 40% of its sales during spring, could be devastated by a local economic downturn during this period.

Discontinuances are the result of many factors, including health and changes in family situations, and can result in voluntary decisions to quit. There are, however, other discontinuances which result from an inability or failure to make the business work. For example, an aspirant entrepreneur may have invested his or her life savings – or income – in a business, only to see losses eliminate the investment.

Areas of risk include incompetence and/or unbalanced experience, especially where owners have little knowledge of the major activities of the business, such as finance, purchasing, selling and production.

Other areas of risk include lack of adequate business records, insufficient stock turnover, uncollected accounts, poor inventory control, lack of finance, improper mark-up, lack of sales, lack of managerial experience, lack of technical knowledge, fraud, and unforeseen disasters. If a fire, burglary or extended strike destroys materials, the loss may result in the business declaring bankruptcy.

Consequently, it is vital in the early stages of planning and development, that the entrepreneur is made aware of the fact that he or she *will* encounter risks.

On a positive note, running your own business can be very rewarding. For example, there is the potential to make a great deal of money, offer a satisfying service to your community and gain prestige. You will find the new challenges and experiences many and varied, and, most importantly, you will have the opportunity to be proud of your achievements. To reap the rewards that success brings, ambition, desire, capital, and keen interest are not enough. You still need a good money-making idea, technical and managerial ability, preparation, experience, perseverance, good judgement, a competitive spirit, and excellent health to carry out all of these.

Many people see a business opportunity as a high-risk speculation. A *true* opportunity *should not* be such a high risk – and will always be obvious in its benefits. And remember, although entrepreneurs are success-oriented, they are not deterred by the possibility of failure.

SUMMARY

It is important that you know what you want, are confident about what success means to you, and are aware of the risks and rewards involved in running an independent business. It is only now that you can begin to set realistic personal and financial goals.

You will need to consider remuneration, working hours, personal/family relationships. You will also need to evaluate the effect on your own psychological needs: will you be working long hours under stressful conditions, and can you cope with this?

You will have to consider whether you need to employ consultants to assist you with planning, and whether there are avenues where you feel less confident and need to employ trained staff to do the work for you.

Social acceptance is also an important aspect: are your family and friends supportive of your idea for a business venture? Are you entering into a business primarily to make money or will the venture also give you a sense of self-fulfilment?

Obviously, your occupation represents much more than just a set of skills and functions: it represents a way of life. It largely provides and determines the environment in which you will work and live, and it selects, and often strengthens, the traits that you use most frequently. There is definite satisfaction in developing and maintaining a successful business.

WHERE WILL YOU WORK?

Several options exist when it comes to choosing the premises from which you will operate your business. You may want to consider working from home, renting or sharing premises, or buying premises. Many factors can influence your decision – for example, the type of business (manufacturing, retail, wholesale or service-related), personal preferences, where your competition is based, geographical restrictions, legal regulations, and, of course, the amount of finance available. Starting-up may also involve designing an appropriate layout for your operations and/or structural changes.

Working from home may be a viable option as the costs involved in renting office space often exceed the entrepreneur's budget. It may be more convenient, especially if your time schedule involves balancing work and domestic responsibilities. Overhead costs, including rent or rates, can be kept to a minimum by converting an area of the house into office and/or storage space. If you decide to work from home, it is advisable to check with your municipality regarding licencing requirements and specific operating regulations. In some cases, it may be impractical to work from home.

When searching for suitable premises remember to take into consideration factors such as parking facilities for staff and clients, the condition of the building, lease requirements, and zoning and licensing regulations. Also check whether cleaning, maintenance and security of the building are provided by the owners, and included in the lease agreement. Another option may be to share facilities with another business. These could include, for example, a secretary, fax machine and photocopier. If the business you share premises with complements your business, you may even pick up some valuable contacts. The entrepreneur, whether setting up a home office or studio or operating from rented or shared facilites, is confronted with the challenge of having to decide on the location of the business. Obviously, this will be influenced by the type of business you have.

The economic base of an area will be a determining factor: the owner will want to locate the business in an area that has an increasing buying power for the goods and services the business offers.

Geographic considerations are important. Most businesses will want to be located close to the market for their goods or services, and the availability of labour in the area is often a factor that has to be taken into consideration. Various codes, ordinances, and deed restrictions often limit the establishment and operation of a business.

The zoning ordinances and subdivision regulations determine where and under what conditions a business may operate. Different municipalities have different regulations. Building, electrical, plumbing, fire, and health codes require that businesses meet certain standards, and various permits and licences may have to be obtained to certify compliance with these codes.

COMPETITION

Competition can be positive or negative, depending on whether the business thrives on it or is destroyed by it. A small business specialising in exclusive babywear opened in a mall and was earning a good profit. Then a large retail outlet, offering a wider range of items, and specialising in budget lines, opened in the same mall. This competition negatively affected the small business, and its owner was obliged to re-evaluate the situation. The options were to introduce items that were not supplied by the competitor or close down.

CHAPTER

4

What form of business?

■

Business Categories

Your Business and Tax

Tax Rebates/Deductions

Licences and Regulations

Contracts

Insurance

■

Enterprise is about making things happen. It refers to the willingness and ability of people to be self-determining and flexible, influencing, shaping and taking control of their lives in every sphere.

The small enterprise is often a source of new materials, processes, ideas, services, products and methods that larger firms are reluctant to provide. While it is obvious that mass production is essential to satisfy consumer demand, there is a growing market for items that are unique, for services designed to meet specific objectives, for products that are individually styled, and for methods that are applied to detailed specifications. The small business is flexible and is able to adjust its production according to these demands for specialization and can, therefore, stimulate efficiency and competitive prices in the industry. Some entrepreneurs operate offices, practices or consulting rooms from home, while others run their businesses in the formal private sector and work from commercial premises. Craftspeople and technical entrepreneurs operate cottage industries from their homes, either providing a service or creating products. Other informal businesses include agencies (such as building maintenance, employment, accommodation and export/import agencies), design studios, playgroups for pre-school children, and translating services. Hawkers and street vendors are regarded as informal traders, selling their goods at flea-markets, door-to-door and at fairs. Artisans such as motor mechanics, plumbers and electricians can generate income by moonlighting, while those with a flair for baking, bottling or catering can supply home-industry shops operating in the formal sector.

BUSINESS CATEGORIES

There are three basic business categories: manufacturing, merchandising (including wholesalers and retailers), and service-oriented concerns.

Manufacturing businesses convert raw materials into useful products. These businesses can follow one of two routes: producing goods for other manufacturers or manufacturing for the consumer market.

Merchandisers deal in the purchase and sale/distribution of products. Products can be sold directly to the retailer or to a wholesaler for resale. Typical retail establishments include pharmacies, furniture stores, cafés, car dealers and service stations.

Service-oriented businesses include, for example, domestic cleaning services, catering businesses, and computer and specialist outlets undertaking machine servicing and repairs.

There has been tremendous growth in service industries over the years, due to the increase in purchasing power of the average consumer. For example, in families where both spouses are employed outside the home, there has been an increase in the amount of money spent on services such as garden maintenance and home cleaning services. Money is also being spent on service-oriented businesses offering leisure activities.

STARTING YOUR OWN BUSINESS

Many people enjoy the challenge and sense of accomplishment that come from creating something new. Some of the motivating factors for starting a new business include the opportunity and freedom of choice to define the nature of your business and create the type of physical surroundings you prefer – even if this means starting on a micro-small level.

Equipment, materials and tools can be selected to suit your business' needs, and use the most recent processes and procedures. As the new business owner, you can obtain fresh inventory, have a free hand in selecting, training and motivating personnel, design and implement your own management information system and select the competitive environment for your business.

It is important to remember that new old-businesses formed by piggy-backing (adapting and/or improving a product or service) have to compete with established businesses doing the same thing, for example, restaurants and clothing boutiques. When making your choice it is worth avoiding existing, often overcrowded markets.

There are also potential disadvantages to establishing your own business. You will have to deal with unproven performance records in sales, service and profits.

Problems may arise in assembling resources, finding suitable premises to operate from, and dealing with the responsibility of selecting and training a new work-force. You may be faced with product line, production, marketing and distribution problems.

And, on the financial side, problems in establishing a basic accounting system and control systems may arise. Alternatively, you could study an established business, improve on its new product, service and production methods and go into competition. Many people enjoy the challenge and sense of accomplishment that come from creating something new.

WHAT TYPE OF BUSINESS?

There are four forms of legal business entity: sole proprietor, partnership, close corporation, and company. Before choosing a particular form of ownership, the entrepreneur should be aware of the benefits and disadvantages of each, and assess which is the most appropriate for his or her proposed business. When in doubt about choosing one of the businesses discussed in this section, seek professional help before committing yourself.

Sole proprietor

A sole proprietor operates a business in his or her own name. If you have the facilities, cash and customers, you can start trading under your own name immediately.

In legal terms, there is no difference between the owner and the business. It is the easiest and least expensive form of business to establish. Unless you intend to register for VAT (which is dependent on your level of income), there are no rules about the records you have to keep and an external audit is not essential. However, it would be wise to keep accurate financial records, as you will have to declare your income to the Receiver of Revenue.

This form of business ownership allows the owner to have direct control and freedom of action – there are no partners or shareholders to be accountable to. *You* are taxed because *you* are the business. If a sole proprietor runs two businesses and incurs a loss in one, this can usually be written-off against the profits of the other.

A sole proprietor has sole responsibility for the business, and, if things go wrong, this can result in several negative aspects.

One of the disadvantages of being a sole proprietor is unlimited liability. The owner is responsible for all debts incurred by the business. All assets and liabilities form part of his/her personal estate. Should a sole proprietor die, the business is regarded as part of the personal estate.

Another negative aspect of being a sole proprietor is that the owner has no access to equity capital. He or she must rely on loans from banks and/or individuals, and any other non-equity sources of finance.

Partnership

There are few restrictions on setting up a partnership. By law, it is defined as an agreement between two or more people (but not exceeding 20) in which each person contributes to an enterprise and benefits from the profits. They also share all the risks. As long as the partnership exists, *all* partners are responsible for *every* aspect of the running of the business.

A partnership is not a separate legal or tax entity, and each partner is taxed in his or her individual capacity on the profits derived from the business.

Partnerships can work very well provided the individuals involved contribute equally in terms of effort and commitment, there is explicit trust between the partners, and a willingness to spend long hours working together.

A 'sleeping partner' is someone who makes capital available, but does not intend playing an active role in the running of the business. He or she can protect him- or herself from joint liability risk by having the partnership registered as a 'limited' partnership. In a partnership, the only people you are accountable to are your partners.

Disadvantages of a partnership are unlimited liability, a lack of continuity and divided authority. All the partners are personally liable for the debts of the business, even if they were incurred through one partner's mismanagement or dishonesty. Death releases a partner from his obligations – but in some cases the estate remains liable. Unless 'public leave' of the partnership is taken, by notifying your business contacts, you will remain liable for all debts incurred by the partnership. It is advisable to have a legal contract drawn up and agreed to by all partners. Such a contract should address the following points:

Profit sharing This should specify how profits and losses are to be shared, and indicate the limits on partners' monthly capital withdrawals.

Responsibilities and duration This stipulates who is responsible for particular tasks. It also sets a limit on the length of time the partnership will operate – either a specific number of years or indefinitely. A cancellation period, for example, three months, can also be decided upon by the partners.

Voting rights Unless otherwise stated, all partners have equal voting rights. It is advisable to define exactly what a policy or voting decision is, and how such decisions are to be made. Consideration must be given to the procedure to be used in expelling or admitting a partner.

Time off Every partner is entitled to a share of the profits – even when ill or on holiday. Guidelines should be compiled on the acceptable length and frequency of holidays, and what action should be taken if a partner is absent for an extended period of time.

Withdrawing capital A decision will have to be made regarding each partner's share of the business capital in the event of the partnership being dissolved.

Accountancy procedures Accounts need not be filed or audited. It may be wise, however, to get partner agreement on an acceptable standard of accounting, and have an external accountant carry out this work. Sleeping partners may insist on this.

Close corporation

A close corporation is regarded as a separate legal entity comprising no more than ten members. It is also regarded as a separate tax entity, and is taxed at the same rate as a company. Many people starting their own business prefer this option as it is simple to establish and requires very little administration. Registration with the Registrar of Close Corporations and Companies is necessary to form a close corporation. By law, the letters 'cc' must appear after the name of the business and its registration number should appear on all correspondenceand cheques.

All the members of a close corporation actively involved in the day-to-day running of the business are accountable to one another. Limited liability is possible with a close corporation. If debts are incurred, individuals are not liable merely by virtue of their membership. All debts are the responsibility of the business – not the individual members.

A close corporation also has the advantage of being able to arrange, for example, a pension scheme, medical aid and provident fund benefits on behalf of its members. The Registrar is entitled to deregister a close corporation if it is lying dormant or if it has no assets or liabilities.

Company

This is the most expensive form of business to establish. Financially, a company is closely regulated and an annual audit by a chartered accountant is a required. Certain administrative procedures are necessary, both in the formation and the daily running of a company, which have to comply with the requirements of the Companies Act. Companies are taxed at a higher rate than individual taxpayers.

A company is an independent legal entity in which the number of shareholders may not exceed fifty. Although controlled by the shareholders, the existence of the company is not threatened by a change of shareholders – all assets, profits and liabilities belong to the company, not to the shareholders. Limited liability is probably the greatest advantage of forming a company.

The existence of a company may be continuous and ownership is transferable. Unlike a partnership, it does not automatically dissolve if one partner dies, nor may it be de-registered if the business is dormant, as in the case of a close corporation.

A company can arrange pension, medical aid and provident fund benefits for its directors and staff.

YOUR BUSINESS AND TAX

SOLE PROPRIETOR AND PARTNERSHIPS

All businesses have to pay tax on profits earned. Anyone trading as a sole proprietor or in a partnership is regarded, by law, as self-employed and taxed as an individual according to the provisional income tax system.

The payment of provisional tax is intended to assist tax-payers in meeting their tax liabilities by way of instalments out of taxable income received during the tax year. It avoids, as far as possible, the need to make provision for substantial lump-sum tax payments at the end of a tax year.

A sole proprietor pays income tax on net profits, that is, *after* allowable expenses have been deducted. Partnerships are taxed in the same way, but each individual is taxed according to his or her *share* of the profits generated by the partnership.

The amount of tax to be paid will be determined by a tax assessor at the Department of Inland Revenue after taking into consideration income, operating expenditure and profit.

CLOSE CORPORATIONS AND COMPANIES

Close corporations and companies are regarded as separate legal entities and must register on their own as tax-payers. The taxable income of close corporations and companies is calculated in a similar way to that of a sole proprietor or partnership, but is based on a set percentage. The tax year coincides with the financial year of the business.

VALUE ADDED TAX (VAT)

If the estimated value of your taxable turnover is likely to be more than R150 000 in any 12-month period, you are obliged to register for VAT within one month of starting your business. VAT is a broad-based consumption tax levied at each point from primary production to final consumption, in instances where value is added to goods and services. The registered vendor is obliged to pay the VAT collected from customers to the Receiver of Revenue every two months.

VAT is payable on the sale of new and used goods, the renting or hiring of goods, the rendering of services and the provision of facilities. Goods that are not VAT taxable include certain items of food.

How does VAT work? Let's look at an example ...

A wholesaler supplies goods to a vendor, at a price inclusive of VAT. This is regarded as the 'input tax' for the vendor. The vendor then resells the goods to the consumer and the price charged includes VAT. This is known as 'output tax'. In other words, the vendor has *paid* input tax and *received* output tax. The difference between the two is the amount due to the Receiver of Revenue. If input tax exceeds output tax, the amount may be claimed from the Receiver of Revenue.

The duties of a vendor, when it comes to VAT, are to charge output tax on all taxable supplies (calculated at selling price), keep all tax invoices received, maintain a proper set of accounts, and issue appropriate tax invoices to clients.

Consult your nearest Department of Inland Revenue for more detailed information regarding taxable supplies and exempt supplies for businesses, who should be registered, accountancy procedures and compliance, tax periods, as well as practical considerations, such as stationery and price display.

TAX REBATES/DEDUCTIONS

Tax *rebates* are determined according to such factors as age and marital status. Tax *deductions* include the following:

- Entertainment expenses (if this is an essential part of your business)
- Medical expenses
- Donations to approved education funds
- Tool allowance
- Financial commitments to educational institutions
- Current and arrears pension fund
- Current and arrears retirement annuity fund (The maximum amount that you may deduct depends on two factors: how much income you earn from non-retirement funding sources, and how much you earn from retirement funding employment.)
- Travel expenses
- Study expenses
- Office-at-home expenses (computer, stationery, postage)
- Enforced membership fees for professional unions
- Accountancy fees
- Expenses normally associated with running a business (wages for domestic worker, messenger, typist)
- Other (for example, depreciation on books, furniture)

If you derive an income from patents, trademarks, copyrights or inventions, you may deduct part of the expenses incurred in developing, producing or buying these rights. If your total expenditure does not exceed R200 per year, you may deduct the full amount.

You may be conducting a bona fide business from home, in which case you are entitled to a percentage rebate of your taxable income for office space, telephone and electricity accounts, wear and tear and all expenses connected with the house (including cleaning, maintenance, insurance, rates and rent – but not capital repayments on your bond). For example, if your study/office occupies 10% of the floor space of your house, you should be able to deduct 10% of the costs from your taxable income.

Many businesses lease their facilities and equipment, rather than buying them, to minimize initial capital outlay. Leasing expenses represent costs of doing business and are therefore tax-deductible. In some instances, however, it is sometimes better to buy than to lease equipment in order to gain a tax advantage or depreciation write-offs.

LICENCES AND REGULATIONS

Many municipalities are following a deregulation policy in a bid to make it easier for people to pursue self-employment. Some local councils require entrepreneurs to have a trade licence, regardless of the type of business or where it operates. Requirements vary from one municipality to another, and it is best to check whether a trading licence is in fact necessary before launching into operation.

A hawker's licence is necessary if you intend selling items at outdoor venues, for example, on the street, outside factories, or running a stall at a flea-market. This can be obtained from your local licensing department for a nominal fee.

If you prepare and sell food, a health inspector and a representative of the fire department will assess the premises to ensure that certain health and safety regulations are met. (This excludes businesses where food is prepared and sold from a private dwelling.)

Regulations regarding health and entertainment facilities have been relaxed, but, according to law, authorities may conduct checks on these establishments at any time.

CONTRACTS

A contract is an agreement between two or more people, and can be either verbal or written. A verbal contract is as legally binding as a written contract, although the latter offers better protection for the parties concerned. A contract ends when everyone concerned has fulfilled their obligations or by agreement. It also ends if one party breaks the contract or dies.

Breach of contract occurs when all the terms and conditions of the contract are not met and legal action can be taken to counter this:

- The court can order the guilty party to do as was promised.
- An interdict can be granted by the court against the defaulting party.
- The wronged party can sue the other for damages.
- The wronged party can cancel the contract and sue for damages if the other party has not carried out an important part of the contract.

WHAT TO LOOK OUT FOR

- Never sign a contract that has blank spaces.
- Always request a copy of any contract you sign.
- Before you sign a contract, make sure that it clearly sets out all the terms and monies to be paid.
- Only sign a contract if you have read and understood everything in it.

INSURANCE

What will happen to my business if ...

... I die or suddenly become incapacitated?
... a fire destroys my business?
... there is pilferage by customers or employees?
... an employee embezzles company funds?
... my business is robbed?

All businesses should have some form of insurance, even if it is only minimal. Some of the major types of insurance to consider include motor vehicle, fire, theft, public liability, workers' compensation, life insurance, business continuation life insurance, and health. It is usually advisable to have an insurance consultant assess your requirements.

CHAPTER

5

WHAT WILL IT ALL COST?

■

BUDGETING

START-UP COSTS

PRICING

PROFITABILITY

MORE PRICING STRATEGIES

HAZARDS OF INACCURATE PRICING

RECORD-KEEPING

■

To establish a feasible retail price which is both customer-oriented and profitable, accurate pricing and costings are essential.

A good place to start is to draw a comparison between your current financial situation and the estimated economic potential of the business you are considering. The earnings that new business owners aspire to will invariably differ from person to person, and from business to business. Also draw a comparison between start-up capital and your potential earnings.

If your business involves manufacturing goods, calculate the number of units you will have to produce and market during one month. Note what each item will cost you to make and add your profit. If you will be providing a service, calculate the number of potential contracts you can close per day. Consider charging by the hour for your services, which will give you an indication of your potential earnings per month. Remember to include basic start-up costs in your calculation.

BUDGETING

A *budget* is a plan that numerically specifies anticipated results and serves as a basis for feedback, evaluation, and follow-up. The sales budget and the cash budget are the two most commonly used forms.

The sales budget is the core from which all other budgets flow. For example, if the owner-manager believes that half the sales for the year are expected during the first three months of the year, half of the production should be completed and ready for shipping during (or soon after) that period. By linking the other budgets to the sales budget, the owner-manager can adjust expenditure accordingly. For example, if sales are higher than anticipated, production can be raised.

The cash budget is also a vital aspect of budgeting. Cash planning should take into consideration the daily and weekly cash requirements for normal operation, as well as the maintenance expenses for that period. The amount of money that is likely to be collected during that time should also be determined.

If a cash shortage is anticipated after comparing expenses and collections, a line of credit may have to be considered.

All entrepreneurs are urged to appreciate the importance of financial management and effective costings. The rewards are worth the effort, for this is how your business idea will survive, grow, develop *and* make money!

START-UP CHECKLIST

- *Rent*
- *Installation of fixtures and equipment for production*
- *Renovating premises*
- *Initial inventory*
- *Legal and other professional fees*
- *Licences and permits*
- *Advertising/promotion*
- *Cash*
- *Accounts receivable (estimate how much will be tied up in receivables by credit customers and for how long, that is, whether it will take 30, 60 or 90 days before you are paid. A certain percentage may have to be written off as uncollectable)*
- *Salaries*
- *Delivery costs*
- *Telephone and other utilities*
- *Insurance*
- *Tax*
- *Maintenance fund (for general upkeep of premises, servicing machines, etc.)*

START-UP COSTS

Every business will have different actual start-up costs. The following list offers a general guideline on factors to be taken into consideration.

Remember that these costs have to be recouped, before a business can begin to reflect profit.

VARIABLE COSTS
Variable costs represent expenses incurred in manufacturing a product or providing a service and change in relation to output. These may include materials, wages, transportation, depreciation, taxes, and advertising costs.

FIXED COSTS
Fixed costs are constant costs, and include rent, heating, lighting, telephone, stationery, postage and some basic professional fees for legal and financial services.

PRICING

The final price of a particular product or service has to be set high enough to cover the actual cost of producing the product (or your time, in the case of a service) and the expenses incurred in selling and distributing them. The price should also include a profit. However, the final price should not be unattainable by customers – the source of sales. A simple formula for pricing is:

Retail price =
Cost/Purchase price + Operating expenses + Profit.

Setting a price is also dependent on the nature of your competition, the perceived value of your product or service, and the actual costs incurred. There are three main approaches to price-setting: competition-based, buyer-based and cost-based.

COMPETITION-BASED

Most entrepreneurs are aware of the price their competitors charge for similar goods and services. Unless there is a very good reason not to, most businesses price with the competition. Not adopting a competition-based approach can lead to an imbalance in the marketplace and is a potential source of conflict within the industry. This type of price-setting strategy is also known as going-rate pricing.

BUYER-BASED

Buyer-based pricing occurs when the market perceives a product to be worthy of a particular price. While this perception may or may not be accurate, the potential buyer is influenced by factors such as promotional marketing and advertising campaigns.

COST-BASED

Cost-based pricing, also known as cost-plus pricing, adds a standard mark-up to the cost of the product.

PROFITABILITY

After taking all the cost factors into consideration, the entrepreneur should calculate whether the profit margin that has been included in the retail price of each unit is indeed profitable and indicates satisfactory financial return on investment.

Three factors need to be considered when calculating profitability – profit margin, sales volume and expenses:

- *Profit margin* – the difference between the retail price and the cost to produce each unit.
- *Sales volume* – the number of units which can be sold over a given period of time. (This figure should be based on thorough market research.)
- *Expenses* – these include all fixed costs incurred over the same period of time.

The amount of actual profit can now be calculated using the profitability formula:

Profit = Profit margin x Sales volume – Expenses

or

Profit =
(Retail price – Cost price) x Sales volume – Expenses

For example, if you buy 100 wooden boxes per month at R30 each, sell all of them at R150 apiece after you have painted and stencilled them, and incur expenses of R2 000, your profit for the month is calculated as follows:

(R150 – R30) x 100 – R2 000 = R10 000

Subsequently, there are four ways in which you can raise your profits:

- Reduce expenses.
- Increase the profit margin by increasing the retail price.
- Increase the profit margin by decreasing the cost price.
- Increase the sales volume by producing and selling more units.

MORE PRICING STRATEGIES

Instances in which the entrepreneur is likely to adopt price-setting strategies include the launching of a new product, and if confronted with the need to adjust prices or to apply discriminatory pricing, psychological pricing, promotional pricing or geographical pricing.

Keep in mind that launching a 'unique' product for which there is no current substitute, allows the entrepreneur to charge what the market will bear. A high price can create and/or support the image of a superior product and maximize profits in the first stage of the product's life-cycle. As substitutes become available, the entrepreneur can adjust the price, thereby maintaining a share of the market. There are several price-setting strategies available to the entrepreneur:

- *Cash discounts* are price reductions given to customers who pay promptly. This benefits the business in terms of improved cash flow and reduced collection costs.
- *Quantity discounts* are price reductions that provide incentive for customers to buy large volumes. For the business this means improved turnover and a reduction in selling, storage and transportation costs.
- *Trade discounts* are offered by manufacturers and suppliers to customers in the trade who handle the business' products. This strategy tends to establish and maintain trade channels and win the loyalty of operators.
- *Seasonal price-setting* is often introduced at the end of a selling season and aimed at 'out of season' customers – for example, sales of summer items to make way for winter items. Businesses have the opportunity to clear old stock, improve liquidity and reduce storage costs.
- *Discriminatory pricing* establishes different market segments and different patterns of demand. It is often aimed at specific customers, such as pensioners and scholars. Price variations can also occur according to location. The benefit of this type of strategy is that the

less desirable selections of product-ranges can still be sold and contribute to turnover and profitability.

- *Psychological pricing* is related to perception – for example, 'the higher the price, the better the product/service'. If the particular product/service price *is* higher than a similar one, it confirms the customer's belief that it has superior qualities or value.
- *Psychological discounting* creates the perception for a customer that he or she is buying a bargain. For example, an item marked R1,99 appears to be cheaper than if it were marked R2,00. The same applies to an item tagged, 'Was R450 – Now only R299'.
- *Promotional pricing* can be divided into: loss leaders and special event pricing. Loss leaders are used to attract customers to buy items that have been priced below cost. At the same time, it is hoped that these customers will buy other 'normally priced' items. Special event pricing is aimed at encouraging customers to buy certain products because of their perceived value. For example, the purpose of sales is twofold – customers are offered bargains while the store is cleared of old stock. Days such as Valentine's Day, Father's Day and Christmas all promote certain products and services because they are perceived to be traditional or customary.

Geographical pricing is aimed at customers living in remote areas. They are expected to pay more for products or services to cover transport/postage and handling costs. To absorb these costs, prices can be set on a regional basis or uniformly on a national basis to allow for varying delivery costs.

HAZARDS OF INACCURATE PRICING

Inaccurate pricing can seriously affect the profitability of a business. Items marked below cost will result in substantial loss, while those marked too high can result in negative sales growth, loss of clientele, and generate doubts about the business' professional standards.

Causes of inaccurate pricing vary. The entrepreneur may have been over-optimistic about the product or under-estimated its popularity.

While most people believe that price reflects quality, a rise in price is nevertheless resented by customers. If, however, this strong conviction of price reflecting quality is adequately reinforced by appropriate marketing effort, the business should show substantial profit. For example, art collectors will expect to pay a high price for an original sculpture by a famous artist; the same philosophy will apply to an individually-styled garment by a well known couturier.

RECORD-KEEPING

Basic record-keeping covers aspects such as legal requirements, quoting and costing, paying accounts, collecting debts, managing cash flow, avoiding losses and planning for growth. For a business to operate efficiently, it is important that these aspects are kept up-to-date, and are essential when overdraft facilities need to be extended, a loan needs to be considered or the business is being sold.

A business financial position is constantly changing. Cash received for sales increases the bank balance; money spent on materials increases the inventory;

machinery decreases in value; goods are processed; and utilities are used. Remember too, that most equipment wears out. For example, a machine costing R7 000 today may be worth nothing in five years' time. Unless it is recorded as a depreciation cost, the business owner may find it difficult to finance the purchase of a new machine if the old one becomes obsolete.

Most entrepreneurs realize that accounting records must adequately and accurately reflect continual changes in assets, liabilities, income, expenses and equity. Street vendors and craftspeople are no less viable entrepreneurs contributing to the national economy than are owner-managers of small businesses in the formal sector. Every entrepreneur should, therefore, foster a professional approach to record-keeping.

Options include employing an accountant on a part-time or full-time basis; many small businesses contract an external accounting agency and find that it is a lot cheaper and efficient. Consult an accountant, the SBDC or your bank for advice on the records you need to maintain and develop your business.

BALANCE SHEET

This can be regarded as a a 'snapshot' of the financial position of the business at any given point in time. Comparisons can be made with previous periods and trends and weak areas can be easily identified.

By definition, the balance sheet always balances. What happens on one side of the balance sheet is offset by something on the other side. Assets will always equal liabilities plus owner's equity.

BREAK-EVEN ANALYSIS

A break-even analysis indicates the point at which your business is running at neither a profit nor a loss. It is the point where a company's sales revenue is equal to its costs of production, and can be expressed either as the number of units to be produced or in rands.

By establishing your break-even point, you can define a definite sales target. It is essential to remember that increased sales do not necessarily mean increased profits. Only when sales exceed the break-even figure, will profits rise with increased sales.

INCOME STATEMENT

This document is also known as a profit and loss statement. Whereas a balance sheet can indicate the financial position of a company at a given point in time, an income statement provides an overview of the business over a particular time span. Income statements that are cast into the future are called *income projections* and are used as forecasting and budgeting tools, estimating future income and expenses. For most small businesses, income projections should cover a three-year period.

CASH FLOW ANALYSIS

Cash flow is the most critical aspect of a new or growing business. Businesses need start-up and growth capital, and a cash-flow analysis indicates:

- How much money will be needed,
- When it will be needed, and
- Where it will come from.

Cash is primarily generated by sales, but not all sales are cash sales. If your business offers credit facilities, your cash flow analysis will indicate when your sales become cash-in-hand.

The cash flow projection reflects ways in which you can finance business operations: for example, by selling some assets, sub-leasing space or offering bigger cash or credit discounts to customers who pay their accounts early or on time. Your business may be subject to some seasonal sales, and again, good cash flow makes the liquidity problems relating to such large, occasional expenses clear.

DEVIATION ANALYSIS

For most small businesses, a one-year cash flow analysis doubles as an operating budget. A budget deviation analysis indicates the extent to which actual financial results differ from budgeted figures. This document allows you to adjust future budget figures if the trend is likely to continue, or to take steps to operate a particular area within the planned budget.

BEWARE OF OVERCAPITALIZING

Many entrepreneurs often overcapitalize on their new or growing businesses. This can lead to a multitude of problems, despite the stock, fixed assets, accounts receivable or rapid growth situation. Operating capital can be rapidly draines by premature purchases of land, buildings, machinery, company cars and expensive vacations.

Where cash shortages do occur, the business owner would be advised to consult an accountant, bank manager, or both. Each will be able to analyze the areas in which cash and costs need to be controlled. On assessment, the entrepreneur may have to reduce stock, collect debts, eliminate unprofitable products and services, re-evaluate renting or leasing arrangements, reduce his or her own salary and perks, and exploit purchase discounts. Obviously, it is preferable to avoid such crises and keep a tight rein on capital expenditure from the outset.

CHAPTER

6

THE BUSINESS PLAN

■

COMPONENTS OF A BUSINESS PLAN

FRONT PAGE

INTRODUCTION

DESCRIPTION OF THE VENTURE

MARKETING STRATEGY

FINANCIAL STRATEGY

FINANCIAL SCENARIOS

OPERATING STRATEGY

APPENDICES

SUMMARY

■

A business plan, simply stated, is a detailed explanation of your business idea. It describes, in writing, the proposed business and its products, services, or manufacturing process. It leads to a sound venture structure, includes a marketing strategy, identifies recognized obstacles, alternative solutions and contingency plans, and serves as your communication tool with all financial and professional sources. It includes other information, such as an analysis of the market, an organizational plan, and measurable financial objectives. It also helps to clarify all aspects of your projected business before you spend too much valuable time and money on it.

Developing a comprehensive business plan is by no means an easy task and may demand a great deal of research to obtain information and ensure that all the details relevant to operating your business are included.

When preparing a business plan, consider the information required by bankers, suppliers, customers, investors and employees. You may need to enrol the services of business consultants, lawyers, bankers, stockbrokers, customers, suppliers and government officials, to help you develop your business plan.

No plan is ever complete and inflexible. Additions or deletions may be necessary. Some things may not work out as expected, while others will have gone unnoticed in the original plan. Reviewing the business plan regularly will allow the entrepreneur to modify his or her approach as and when this is necessary. As an operating tool, your business plan helps you to establish reasonable objectives, forecasts and a description of the business – that is, *what* it will do, *how* it will operate and *why* you think it is viable.

COMPONENTS OF A BUSINESS PLAN

Plans vary in content. Those written to accompany an application for a bank loan tend to contain a great deal of financial information, whereas those prepared for the purpose of managing a business will emphasize operational areas.

In each part of the plan, the entrepreneur is expected to describe operations that have to be caried out and then address the major issues likely to be confronted.

The business plan will be used by prospective investors to evaluate the potential success of your business. It should always be neatly presented, comprehensive, logical, easy to read, and based on fact wherever possible. You will also find that a thorough business plan automatically becomes a complete financing proposal.

MINI-PROPOSAL

A mini-proposal should be drafted in tandem with the comprehensive business plan. It is a short summary of the business plan which can be sent to potential investors to determine levels of interest in the venture. If investors are interested, they will request a complete business plan.

Include:

- *Amount of capital required*
- *Type of industry*
- *Nature of the business*
- *Financial (sales and profit) projections*
- *Staff/management composition and qualifications*

FRONT PAGE

In preparing a professional-looking front page, ensure that it reflects the following information:

- Name of the business (and logo, where appropriate)
- Type of business
- Name/s of the owner/s
- Address/es and telephone number/s of the owner/s
- Date of presentation

INTRODUCTION

The introduction should be concise and stimulate interest in your business proposition. It must include a brief description of the service or product offered, clearly describe the potential of the venture, and state why it is viable. Any distinctive features should be emphasised, and short-, medium- and long-term objectives included.

DESCRIPTION OF THE VENTURE

The purpose of this section is to explain *what* your business is, *how* you are going to run it and *why* you think your business will be successful. Broadly outline the structure of your business; describe its background (including operating history if this is appropriate), nature, form and purpose.

The nature of the product/service offered must be defined, and details of what makes it better than others should be emphasised. Provide a detailed description of your product/service, including photographs and/or drawings where this is appropriate. A detailed description of your production plan, the location, size and cost of business premises (with a diagrammatic layout, if available) can be included in this section. Also detail machinery and equipment requirements, storage and distribution methods, production capacity, stock control procedures, quality control measures and staff requirements and availability. Consider the location of competitors in relation to your business. If a production process is involved, discuss the type of engineering or design support that will be needed. Clarify whether the product parts will be manufactured or simply assembled.

Provide an analysis of the industry, considering your competitors, suppliers, possible substitutes and potential customers. Cover aspects such as uses, unique characteristics, warranties, profit margins, costs, patent protection, technological advantages, research and development, product liability, and market potential.

Also cover the extent and costs involved in further research, testing and development, and ensure that the estimated costs are reasonable. Explain carefully what has already been accomplished (prototype, laboratory testing, early development). Mention any research or technical assistance that has been provided.

Venture description checklist

- type of business/industry analysis
- type of opportunity (for example: new, part-time, expansion, seasonal, year-round, existing)
- viability and growth potential
- detailed description of product/s or service/s
- photographs and/or drawings
- unique characteristics/differentiating factors
- technological advantages
- research and development
- manufacturing details
- patent protection
- warranties
- personal experience
- staffing requirements
- consultants' responses
- prospective suppliers
- financial considerations

MARKETING STRATEGY

A comprehensive, well-thought-out marketing strategy will help to convince investors of the accuracy of your sales projections. You will also have to provide details of any advertising or promotion plans.

How will you advertise, price and distribute your product/service? Be specific (and realistic) about your goals, objectives and time scales, and consider the strengths, weaknesses, opportunities and threats that may be encountered.

It is important to identify your target market, market position and market share. Evaluate all of your competitors and state exactly why and how you will be better. Acknowledge the market sources, studies and assistance used to confirm your statements.

Describe the trends, size and growth potential of the market. You will have to incorporate evidence of a need for your prospective product or service. Then define your customers – who they are and why they will buy your product/service. Your market/customer profile should also identified. How does your competition market its product/service?

A thorough market study should provide all the information you need to complete this section. Summarise and present these market opinions to support your business plan.

Marketing strategy checklist

- identify potential customers
- indicate size of the market
- ways of attracting and keeping this market
- ways of expanding market
- anticipated market share

- competitors
- your competitive edge
- SWOT analysis
- advertising/promotion
- justification of price for product/service
- distribution methods
- methods of financing sales
- sales-force organization

FINANCIAL STRATEGY

In this section of your business plan, statements (either actual or estimate) showing your funding sources and projected expenditure should be supplied. Include a balance sheet, an indication of your break-even point, capital expenditure estimates, and a detailed cash flow statement – all for a projected 12-month period.

Calculate and present an estimated budget. Break this down into the various segments of financing so that investors can evaluate your strategy. For example, an entrepreneur wanting to operate a restaurant will break down his or her budget as follows:

- Purchasing/renting suitable premises
- Refurbishing
- Personnel and training
- Marketing, promotion, printing of menus, etc.
- Contracts with suppliers

Indicate the extent of your own financial contribution and then clearly detail the financing you require (and how you intend using it), and what form of security is available.

Provide a detailed income statement for the following 12 months, and estimated financial forecasts (with your projected month-by-month budget) for the next five years. Refer to data from the industry which would corroborate your estimates.

Be realistic and accurate in your projections. Inaccurate calculations could result in insufficient financing – one of the prime causes of business failure. Areas of major expenditure should be supported by copies of contracts, lease and/or purchase agreements, or similar documents, and appended to the plan.

Also include a capital equipment list (equipment used to manufacture a product, provide a service, or to sell or deliver merchandise), and a record of depreciable assets. Ensure that your reserve for the replacement of capital equipment does not become too low.

Financial strategy checklist

- estimated income for the first year
- start-up costs
- monthly cash flow
- personal financial needs
- total financial needs
- sales volume required for profit
- break-even point
- assets and liabilities
- funding sources
- security available
- allocation of the loan or investment (working capital, new equipment, inventory, supplies, etc.)
- inventory purchases

- specific model name and/or number of each purchase, and price
- amount paid/to be paid in sales tax, installation charges, and/or freight fees
- down-payments on the purchase of, or deposit on the lease for, business premises
- fixture or renovation costs
- lease agreements
- utility installation fees
- stationery costs
- taxes and licenses
- professional services (accountant, attorney, consultant)
- advertising and promotion
- insurance
- travel expenses

Financial scenarios

Include in your business plan the possible results of different scenarios. For example:

- What if turnover drops by 5%?
- What if expenses increase by 10%?
- What if gross profit drops by 3%?
- What if turnover drops by 10% and expenses increase by 6%?

Discuss potential risks *before* investors point them out, for example, price cutting by competitors, any potentially unfavourable industry-wide trends, design or manufacturing costs in excess of estimates, sales projections not achieved, product development schedule not met, difficulties or long lead times encountered in procuring parts or raw materials, or increased innovation and development costs to stay competitive. Ensure that you provide contingency plans. Identify potential problems and obstacles, calculate risks, and present alternative courses of action. Consider the following:

- *How concentrated is your customer base?*
  The fewer the customers, industries or geographic locations you serve, the greater the impact of unexpected events will be.
- *How strong is your financial position?*
  If you can cope with unexpected default by your largest customer, and are comfortable with your sales, your need for credit insurance may be limited. Do you borrow on receivables?
- *How much do you reserve for bad debt?*
  If you have a fairly large reserve, you may need less insurance.
- *What is your profit margin?*
  If a company sells high-margin products/services, it may be able to absorb unexpected losses more easily than a company operating on a tight margin.

OPERATING STRATEGY

This section of the business plan indicates the staffing requirements of the business. It should detail the number and type of employees to be recruited and how you intend recruiting them. Details of working hours, overtime, salaries and benefits should be presented.

The following details should be supplied for each member of the management team:

- Business background
- Managerial experience
- Education level
- Personal information (age, where they live/have lived, special abilities, skills and interests, reasons for going into business)
- Reasons for feeling confident about the venture

Advise potential investors of any steps you have taken or are taking to overcome weaknesses in your management team. If you utilise your business plan to its fullest extent, it will make you fully aware of management strengths and weaknesses.

Also describe the legal structure of your venture. Include an organizational chart, a description of each position's responsibilities and identify any external professional assistance, for example, attorneys, accountants and tax consultants, you consult.

Operating strategy checklist

- How many employees will you need?
- What will their duties be?
- What skills must prospective members of your management team and staff have?
- Will you need to train them? On-the-job training? External training?
- What will training cost the business (in terms of time and money)?

- Are the people you need available? On a full-time or part-time basis?
- What is your policy regarding overtime?
- What are your plans for employee salaries and benefits?
- What are your plans for management compensation and incentives?
- Who will manage the business?
- What qualifications do you have?
- What specialists will you need to consult?
- Why will you need them?
- What legal form of ownership will you choose? Why?

APPENDICES

If you have referred to any of the following documents, they should form part of the appendix at the end of your business plan:

- documents, drawings, agreements
- references, advisers or technical sources
- projections
- legal structure of business
- resumés
- financial statements
- market surveys
- organizational chart

SUMMARY

The business plan summary is a road-map for the would-be entrepreneur, as it pinpoints the objectives of the business. The why, how, where and when of your business should form the basis of this summary.

It is one of the most crucial parts of your business plan as it is your last chance to capture the reader's attention by being positive and enthusiastic about your proposed business venture.

CHAPTER

7

SOURCING FINANCE

■

BANK LOANS

SBDC FINANCE

INFORMAL SECTOR LENDING

INSURANCE POLICIES

CREDIT

TURN-AROUND BUSINESS

■

One of the first questions the small-business owner must confront is, 'Where will the money to start the business come from?' If this question can be answered, the next one will be 'After the initial funds are exhausted, where can extra money be raised?' Remember, it is not enough for a small business to get started – it must be able to survive for at least six months without the need for additional funds. Until sufficient capital is available, the entrepreneur is not ready, financially, to launch the venture.

Small-business owners often need to borrow money for various reasons: for example, to start up, on research and development, for expansion/relocation, to start exporting. Access to finance, or the lack of it, is one of the main flashpoints between small business and financial institutions. While banks are by no means the only source of finance available, your bank manager is a good starting point.

The legal way in which you intend to establish your business (or have established your business) will significantly influence the form of finance available to you. Before approaching a financial institution for business-related capital, the aspirant entrepreneur should assess his or her attitude to the business venture:

- Is the potential success of the business worth risking your life savings for?
- Are you prepared to commit yourself fully to the business venture?
- Are your prepared to work seven days a week, 14 hours a day?
- Will your business take top priority in your life?
- Do you have the total support of your family?

- Is your health good?
- Can you cope with constant stress?
- Are you aware of the fact that the majority of new businesses will fail?

Your answer should be 'Yes' to all of these questions.

Certain objective criteria need to be met before applying for finance:

- The purpose for which the funds are sought must be the pursuit of profit through commerce, the manufacture and supply of goods, and/or the provision of services.
- You should never have been liquidated, sequestrated or compromised with your creditors, nor should you have been involved in any form of dishonest conduct. (Details of sequestration and liquidation will be required if applicable.)
- You must be the majority shareholder of the business, be entitled to the bulk of its profits, and be employed on a full-time basis by the business. Equal partnerships, close corporations and companies apply for finance in the name of the business. The part-time entrepreneur can apply for a personal loan.
- You should have completed some formal training in order to undertake this type of business or have a minimum of two years' experience in the type of business envisaged.
- You must be prepared to cede your assets as security.
- The funds should be used in the establishment of a new business venture or for expansion of a current business venture.

BANK LOANS

Recently, the attitudes of major banking institutions have become more positive towards small business. They offer a wide range of services, including overdrafts, term loans, trade bill finance, factoring, leasing, import/export finance and equity financing.

The bank will examine exactly what you want the money for, and whether the business venture is indeed viable – and they will want to know when the loan can be paid back.

Repayment periods vary, depending on the type of loan and what the money is being used for. Remember that working capital (salaries, overheads, and equipment) will be required during the first three or four months of operation and that this amount may not be covered by your income during that time. Overdraft facilities or short-term loans may be available for this.

In reviewing your application for a loan, your bank manager will examine your business plan to determine the structure of your business, whether it is capable of adapting to changes in the economic environment, your management expertise, your sources of payment, the money you are prepared to invest, and the amount of finance requested. Your balance sheet, and assets and liabilities will be analyzed. The bank will also conduct its own valuation and consider factors such as the net-value of your assets and whether these assets are easily realized. The value of any insurance policies, fixed deposits, shares and unit trusts will also be reviewed.

Remember that when repaying a loan, you will be faced with interest charges in addition to capital repayments.

Your application for finance may be turned down for various reasons, for example:

- Your plan may appear unrealistic or a high risk.
- Insufficient collateral.
- Your business plan may not supply enough detail on which a decision can be based.
- Your character and financial stability may be dubious.

While there is no law in South Africa that obliges a bank to give reasons for turning down a loan application, nothing prevents you from requesting your bank manager to discuss the factors that worked against you.

Remember, many entrepreneurs who do not have any assets but who have very good business ideas, and who are prepared to invest a little money in themselves, have been successful in obtaining financing.

SECURED LOANS

Secured loans are backed by collateral (for example, property, savings accounts and investments). Taking liens over assets ties the borrower to the deal, and ensures that he or she is fully committed to the new venture. Should a business venture fail, the assets pledged will be retained by the lender as a way of recovering monies owed.

UNSECURED LOANS

Unsecured loans are not backed by collateral. They are mostly short-term loans and are only available to creditworthy applicants. The loan is supported by the lender's faith in the borrower's ability to repay the loan.

OVERDRAFT

The most popular short-term loan is an *overdraft*. It is simple to arrange and sums of money can be drawn within the agreed limit. It is a short-term loan intended to finance short-term needs, for example, working capital, dealing with seasonal peaks and troughs, supplementing cash flow and personal needs. Interest is paid only on the outstanding daily balance. Of course, interest rates can fluctuate, so what is a small amount of money one year can be crippling the next, if interest rates rise dramatically.

Overdrafts are, theoretically, repayable on demand, so it is advisable *not* to use this particulr facility to finance long-term needs.

TERM LOANS

Term loans (short-, medium- and long-) are more formal arrangements than an overdraft. Financing methods for term loans include mortgages, flexi-bonds, loan finance, long-term leasing and hire purchase. They cover periods of up to three years, three to ten years and ten to twenty years respectively. It should be noted, however, that banks will only grant long-term loans to small businesses in exceptional cases.

These types of loans are usually secured against an existing fixed asset or one to be acquired, or are guaranteed personally by the proprietors. This may involve lawyers' or consultants' fees for legal representation and specialist counselling. The interest rates on these loans can either be fixed for the term or vary according to the prevailing interest rate. Most hire-purchase contracts are medium-term loans.

SUSPENSIVE SALE AND LEASING AGREEMENTS

In terms of *suspensive sale*, tangible business assets, such as vehicles and equipment, are purchased by a financier and sold to the business. The goods can be repaid over a period of up to five years.

Depending on the projected profitability and therefore tax liability of the business, consideration could be given to *leasing* rather than suspensive sale agreements. Advice on the best option for your business can be obtained from your bank.

SMALL BUSINESS UNITS

Most of the major banking institutions have small business units. These operate specifically in the interests of entrepreneurs by providing loans, account packages and specialist consultation services.

SBDC FINANCE

The Small Business Development Corporation offers the following financing options:

- Bridging finance
- Contract finance
- Equity finance
- Instalment sale finance
- Loan guarantees through participating banks
- Term loans
- Venture capital for technology development

The SBDC's *General Finance Programme* is aimed at new and existing business ventures which, apart from financing, require limited additional support.

Small business start-up finance is available for entrepreneurs who are either starting up for the first time or expanding their products or services. Recovery finance is intended for businesses in difficulty – those whose continued existence is jeopardized by circumstances beyond their control and in need of high levels of support. Bridging finance is available for businesses requiring ready cash to finance contracts until payments are received.

The *Comprehensive Assistance Programme* provides for the special requirements of informal and semi-formal enterprises. Support services are combined with financing to ensure a comprehensive package for the entrepreneur. Support services include advice, training and counselling on administration, bookkeeping, buying, management, merchandising, marketing, pricing and record-keeping.

The *Mini-loan Programme* provides for the needs of micro-enterprises which usually need money urgently on a short-term basis.

Interest rates charged by the SBDC are comparable to those of other lending institutions. Repayment terms are determined by the estimated cash flow of the enterprise and the type of asset being financed – for example, working capital (one to three years), machinery and equipment (three to five years), fishing vessels (three to ten years), land and buildings (five to twelve years).

The following are some of the requirements that need to be met for a loan to be granted:

- The business must be economically viable and have potential.
- The business must be profit-oriented.
- The applicant must have management and technical expertise suited to the type of operation.

- The return on assets or investments must cover the finance charges.
- Security or collateral must be provided.
- The project must create jobs.
- The business must be located in South Africa.
- The business must be independently owned.

INFORMAL SECTOR LENDING

With established lending institutions often failing to cater for micro-loans needed by informal traders, this sector has now created finance schemes such as *stokvels* and savings clubs, and retail lending institutions can provide micro-loans of between R100 and R5 000 without the need for collateral.

The Small Enterprise Foundation (SEF), the Get Ahead Foundation (GAF), the Independent Business Enrichment Centre, and the Women's Bank are part of what is fast becoming a vibrant financial market.

STOKVEL

A stokvel *refers to a common fund; monthly instalments are paid into a collective fund, from which members can borrow. One of the group's members is appointed as the 'lender'. First-time borrowers can draw a minimum amount. When this amount has been repaid, the next loan that they apply for may be increased. For example, if the first loan amounts to R700, the next one may be R1 000. Any outstanding payments are recovered from previous payments made into the fund. In most cases, however, members realize that it is in their best interests to ensure that they continue paying each month. The process of 'rotating' the money as a result of non-payment, proportionately reduces the amount that particular member is able to borrow from the fund. Rotating the money is a very effective incentive for prompt and regular payment as small and informal traders, who often cannot obtain loans from major institutions, depend on this line of credit and do not want it terminated. Some organizations also insist on the group having its own savings account and records must be produced at meetings as proof that the money has been banked.*

INSURANCE POLICIES

Insurance policies are often regarded as viable sources of financing. Members who have been contributing to life insurance policies, endowment policies and savings policies for over two years are entitled to surrender, borrow against, or cede the policy to a bank as collateral. Entrepreneurs should, however, consider retaining a portion of the policy to ensure insurance cover, and continue with contributions.

CREDIT

The business world could not operate without credit. 'Buy now, pay later' is what credit is all about. Trade credit is extended from one business to another, and almost always carries a discount for prompt payment.

Manufacturers and suppliers often grant credit to distributors, dealers, and direct buyers, while retailers and service-oriented ventures may offer credit on their services. This allows the customer (or entrepreneur) to purchase goods and pay for them at an agreed future date. For manufacturers, credit facilities often mean advance orders.

A retail or service firm may choose to have its own charge account plan, or may use a bank card plan, to attract customers who then have a choice as to their method of payment. Most of the individual company cards carry no service charge to customers who pay their monthly balances promptly. The entrepreneur with 'good credit' is placed on a preferred list for automatic approval within certain credit limits. There are several types of consumer credit facility:

Open credit allows a customer to 'charge it' to an account, which must be honoured according to a predetermined arrangement, for example, 30-days, six months, or on presentation of the account.

Revolving credit can often result in eternal indebtedness. With this type of credit, a business can set a limit to the amount that may be charged, and any purchase below this is automatically approved for credit sale. The customer then pays a specific amount or percentage of the total charges at the end of each month. Interest is charged each month on the unpaid balance, while credit purchases can still be made up to the limit.

Instalment accounts require a customer to make a down payment, usually around 20% of the total purchase price, with the balance spread over a specified monthly payment plan.

Budget accounts are designed to facilitate purchases that ordinarily fall between short-term open accounts and longer-term instalment accounts. The total debt is usually paid off in equal instalments. Service charges are only levied when the customer defaults on the payment plan.

TURN-AROUND BUSINESS

A business that has not lived up to its expectations often finds itself struggling and has difficulty in obtaining financing. When an entrepreneur needs capital to finance a turn-around, he or she must think of the venture as a new business. Pretend that you are starting all over again, except this time you have a thorough knowledge of the past and new insight into your old mistakes.

Three major steps must be followed:

IDENTIFY THE COMPANY'S PROBLEMS

It is generally best to call in external help because the business owner and managers are often 'too close to the wood to see the trees'. Ask your accountant, lawyer or business consultant to help you identify the problems.

FIND A WAY TO SOLVE THE PROBLEMS

You need a plan of action that details how you can save your company from bankruptcy. A turn-around business plan must include a detailed explanation of the company's past. Be truthful, include the good *and* the bad points – financial sources will respect your integrity. Provide details of what went wrong and why, what you have learned from your mistakes, and what you plan to do to prevent the same problems recurring. Your banker, accountant or lawyer can refer you to consultants who specialize in turn-around businesses.

SOLVE THE PROBLEMS

Start solving your problems *now* – not after you get the money. You won't be able to raise money until you have begun to turn the business around. In other words, you can't say, 'I plan to do this and that'; you must be able to say, 'I am doing this and that, *with this result*'.

Take a fresh look at every angle of the business: examine all the costs, profit margins, sales and marketing techniques. It is essential that you approach the new venture with an enthusiastic attitude. Only once your plan is complete, is it time to look for financing.

FINANCING FOR TURN-AROUND BUSINESS

As mentioned previously, this is one area is which raising finance is not easy – you must be able to prove that something has changed or will change to improve the business in the future. The first objective when relying on internal capital sources should be cash management – that is, to produce cash *in* the company. This could involve selling off assets that do not contribute to current earnings, for example, unused equipment. Alternatively, patents and trademarks could be licensed to other companies. Even sub-leasing space to another company produces immediate cash. Cash can also be drawn from managing receivables. Collection techniques could be improved – for example, bigger discounts could be offered if accounts are paid early or on time. Major customers may even be prepared to advance cash in return for better prices or exclusivity in their territories or market. Similarly, suppliers and vendors should be consulted in an attempt to arrange better terms so that you can continue to buy from them. Emphasis should also be placed on reducing costs wherever possible. The final key to cash management is improving sales – the essence of a turn-around – and may involve hiring new salespeople or management to give a boost in this area. Once you have exhausted all the potential internal capital sources, start pursuing external sources. Begin with traditional institutions such as banks and other asset-based lenders. A good turn-around business plan is critical here: your potential backers will want to see what has been learned from past mistakes.

CHAPTER

8

MARKETING, PROMOTION AND ADVERTISING

■

THE MARKETING MIX

USING AN AGENCY

YOUR OWN STRATEGY

ADVERTISING THE PRODUCT/SERVICE

MARKETING OPTIONS

■

Marketing not only plays an important role in the day-to-day running of a business, but also in its long-term development, and requires multi-dimensional objectives beyond mere cost-per-sale. The emphasis of marketing is to satisfy the needs, attitudes and lifestyles of consumers. In spite of its importance, marketing is frequently an area that is neglected by the entrepreneur.

One of the most important things the entrepreneur needs to understand about the marketing of goods and services, is the market itself. This knowledge is fundamental to pricing, effective advertising strategies, selling and the granting of credit.

The South African market changes constantly and what occurs in the marketplace can determine the success or failure of a business.

THE MARKETING MIX

Creating what is known as the marketing mix – just the right combination of product, place, promotion and price – for your target market is one of the keys to running a profitable business. Some experts have added to the list of marketing activities: distribution, image, positioning, lifestyle, branding, innovation and black/ethnic marketing segmentation.

All business owners are constantly exposed to differing economic climates, changing technology, and even social pressures. Consequently, marketing and advertising plans, whether you use an advertising agency or work out your own strategy, are essential to let the consumer know what product or service you have to offer.

USING AN AGENCY

While most entrepreneurs plan and execute their own marketing and advertising programmes, some will agree that the money paid to hire a public relations/advertising consultancy to do the work on their behalf, is money well spent.

An agency's skilled advertising specialists can assist in developing, implementing and evaluating your advertising plan, can conduct a study of the product or service to determine its advantages and disadvantages relative to those of competitors, and can analyse your present and potential markets in terms of location, season, trade and economic conditions. An advertising agency will also study the various distribution channels for your particular product or service and evaluate the best method of exposing it to the market.

An agency can also help in areas such as package design, sales research, the preparation of sales and service literature, merchandising displays, public relations and publicity, and can arrange to promote the business through product launches, press conferences, interviews and media coverage.

YOUR OWN STRATEGY

Not everyone can afford to hire the services of an agency. Entrepreneurs who intend executing their own marketing and advertising programmes should possess some basic knowledge of marketing options. These include:

- Sending press releases about your product or service to magazines and newspapers.

- Offering prizes or discounts in an innovative way, for example through a competition or lucky draw.
- Making sure that the name of your business is highly visible – at the business premises, on company vehicles, by contributing sponsorship to a specific event, by distributing promotional gifts bearing your company's name.
- Offering customers the best possible service. Apart from being professional, it will encourage word-of-mouth recommendations.
- Producing and circulating information sheets or pamphlets with details of the business and the product/service offered.
- Exhibiting at trade fairs, open days, flea-markets and street-markets.
- Advertising though various mediums – magazines, newspapers, radio, etc.
- Ensuring that every item you produce has a label attached to it, clearly indicating the business' name and address.

The best medium to use will depend on your target customers. Once you have determined who is going to buy your product or service, and where they live, it is relatively easy to establish the best media form to reach them.

ADVERTISING THE PRODUCT/SERVICE

Advertising performs many functions, the most important of which is informing potential buyers of a product or service. While it is imperative that the actual advertisement is truthful at all times, and presented tastefully, it has to be supported by excellent workmanship and reliable customer service. A planned, continuous advertising programme is often more successful than a once-off advertisement.

When it comes to newspaper advertisements, find out if and when special features or supplements are planned. Do any of these relate to your particular product or service? If so, make sure it's seen. It may be to your business' benefit to advertise regularly on a specific page. For example, if your business involves manufacturing tracksuits, an advertisement on a sports page may increase your exposure to your target market.

Radio advertising offers the entrepreneur mass consumer coverage of all ethnic and population groups, either on a national or a regional basis. Regional broadcasting offices can assist the entrepreneur with the various aspects of producing a radio commercial, including scriptwriting and music/jingle composition.

You may also want to consider designing and compiling printed leaflets and brochures. Knock-and-drops can be very economical to produce and can achieve saturation advertising in specific areas at very short notice.

MARKETING OPTIONS

Direct marketing is visible on most television channels on a daily basis. Commodities such as car-care products, household appliances and fitness apparatus are advertised, and viewers are invited to telephone their orders through to a direct marketing company. *Telemarketing* is another form of direct marketing that is receiving greater attention from marketers than it used to. No entrepreneur can afford to subject customers to the boredom of silent 'on hold' time.

You may want to consider running pre-recorded 'messages' over the telephone whenever customers are on hold. These messages can sell specific products or services and alert callers to various accomplishments and changes that have taken place or are going to take place. The best messages inspire questions and enquiries from callers as these can increase the possibility of potential sales. The messages should be revised on a regular basis so that regular callers don't hear the same message over and over again.

Direct mail takes the form of promotional literature which is sent, by post, to potential customers. The direct mail 'package' includes either a pamphlet, brochure or catalogue, and an order form. *Fax-mail* is also becoming a popular means of reaching potential customers.

Consignment selling occurs when a retailer agrees to display merchandise and handle sales in exchange for a percentage of the profits. The retailer does not pay the supplier until the goods are sold, and has the right to return all unsold merchandise to you. While this system relieves the entrepreneur of the responsibility of distribution, it also means that goods can be tied up for long periods of time before you receive payment. The entrepreneur will also be entirely dependent on the consignment retailer to promote and display items, and any that are broken or soiled in the store will be returned to you as a loss. Be sure to confirm all the terms of agreement before selling on consignment. There are many opportunities for *export marketing* – exporting local goods to other countries. If you operate as an export agent, the link between the local supplier and the foreign buyer, there are many options available: representing a domestic manufacturer, buying goods on consignment and dealing direct with foreign buyers, or producing and marketing your own commodities.

CHAPTER

9

Personnel

Recruiting

Interviewing

On-the-Job Training

Interaction and Morale

Employee Tax and Benefits

Often, what starts out as a one-person business, develops and grows beyond expectations, and the need to employ additional staff arises. At this point, the entrepreneur will become involved in personnel recruitment and management. Staffing requirements can usually be anticipated by assessing the needs of the company over a projected period of six to twelve months. To do this successfully, the entrepreneur will have to examine current operations and foreseeable work requirements, and attempt to predict the potential turnover rate. The following questions will need to be considered:

- Can the work be carried out by the present work force or is there a need for additional staff?
- Would a current employee be suitable for the position, or is it necessary to recruit externally?
- Should staff be recruited on a full-time basis?

RECRUITING

After assessing the staffing requirements of the business, the entrepreneur will have to turn his or her attention to defining the job specification for each vacancy and organize a recruiting campaign. Apart from classified newspaper advertisements, potential applicants can often be recruited through trade schools, business colleges and universities.

Employment agencies can be very helpful in locating potential applicants. They will conduct initial screenings of candidates and send only those who have the required qualifications for interviews. Although the agencies charge a fee for their services, this is often money well spent.

INTERVIEWING

Before conducting a formal interview, the applicant should be requested to provide details of his or her background, training and experience (if this is applicable). During the interview, the entrepreneur will have to establish whether:

- the applicant has the right temperament and personality for the job.
- the applicant will need to demonstrate his or her ability by means of a test.
- a medical examination is a required.

INTERVIEWER'S ASSESSMENT

The following assessment schedule may be used to evaluate an applicant's abilities.

- *Education:* *poor* ☐ *fair* ☐ *good* ☐ *outstanding* ☐
- *Work experience:* *none* ☐ *fair* ☐ *good* ☐ *outstanding* ☐
- *Personality:* *antagonistic* ☐ *shy* ☐ *bold* ☐ *likeable* ☐ *pleasing* ☐
- *Communication:* *poor* ☐ *fair* ☐ *clear/efffective* ☐ *concise* ☐
- *Mental alertness:* *slow* ☐ *reasonable* ☐ *quick* ☐ *sharp* ☐
- *Reasoning:* *irrational* ☐ *clear* ☐ *logical* ☐
- *Sincerity:* *doubtful* ☐ *average* ☐ *frank/honest* ☐
- *Enthusiasm:* *pessimistic* ☐ *apathetic* ☐ *optimistic* ☐
- *Determination:* *weak* ☐ *easily discouraged* ☐ *average* ☐ *tenacious* ☐
- *Health:* *poor* ☐ *average* ☐ *excellent* ☐
- *Appearance:* *untidy* ☐ *needs improvement* ☐ *clean/neat* ☐
- *Potential:* *below average* ☐ *average* ☐ *above average* ☐

- *Physical handicaps (if any):* ______________________________

____

- *Additional remarks:* ______________________________

____

____

- *Recommendation:* *recommended for employment* ☐
  need not be considered ☐

The applicant's references should be checked for accuracy and additional information. If the screening process is carried out properly, the entrepreneur should be in a position to select the most suitable candidate.

The entrepreneur will have to make a new employee feel at home in the organization through a job orientation or induction programme. This will include introducing the new person to the rest of the staff and showing how his or her job fits in with the business' overall objectives.

A training programme should form part of every business plan. This should include a statement of the actual training needs and goals, reasons for choosing particular methods, and indicate how results will be evaluated. In addition to on-the-job training, the following are available:

- A conference or structured discussion.
- Lectures. For example, staff knowledgeable in a specific field can attend a lecture on developments, new methods or trends, with the aim of upgrading their levels of competence.
- Role-playing – learning by seeing and doing.
- Programmed instruction (often where the trainee learns at his or her own pace).
- Job rotation.

ON-THE-JOB TRAINING

This type of training is the most practical of all methods suitable for small businesses. It is used for specific job training, such as showing someone how to run a computer, operate a machine, and so on.

The first step involves breaking down the job into its various tasks – as they are performed in practice. This can be done, in writing, with a job break-down sheet which may be kept for future reference as a training aid.

Irrespective of whether on-the-job training is carried out within a few hours or several weeks, four distinct steps should be followed:

1. PREPARATION

The trainer must determine what the trainee already knows about the job before proceeding to assess what the individual still needs to learn. One way of determining this is to set the trainee a skills test and by asking questions, gradually progressing to more advanced interpretations of the specific field.

2. DEMONSTRATION

Here the trainee should be shown the elemenets of how the job is done. As each step is being demonstrated, the trainer should invite the trainee to ask questions about the procedures and, in turn, test the trainee's understanding of the individual tasks by asking questions. For example, if the demonstration involves showing the trainee how to operate a computerized conveyer-belt, the trainer is expected to show the trainee how the job is done, determine the trainee's level of competence in performing the tasks by setting him or her a skills test, and by asking relevant questions to ascertain the trainee's level of understanding. The type of questions asked by the trainee will also give the trainer an indication of the trainee's potential and aspirations.

3. APPLICATION

At this stage the trainer should stand aside and allow the trainee to demonstrate the procedure. When the trainee is carrying out the process correctly, praise should be given. If however, the trainee is unsure of the process, the trainer should step in and demonstrate how to correct the situation. Mistakes should be pointed out and advice given as to how the error can be avoided.

4. INSPECTION

This is where the trainer checks what has been done and evaluates it. The evaluation should be a positive one. If however, the trainee does not fare well in the evaluation, but is sufficiently motivated to learn the necessary skills, the trainer should reassess the training programme. Study material should be made available to encourage self-study, and the trainee given the opportunity to apply his or her new knowledge. Once the trainer is satisfied that the trainee has progressed to the desired level, on-the-job training can be resumed.

INTERACTION AND MORALE

The continual development of effective communication, and staff and management skills, is necessary in order to bring about supportive group morale in an organization, irrespective of its size and type. It is particularly necessary in areas of leadership, communication, motivation, performance evaluation and employee compensation.

Communication could take the form of regular, inspirational pep talks or mind-mapping sessions. A weekly improvement plan could be initiated. By asking yourself, 'How can I do better?' your creative power is switched on and ways for doing things will tend to suggest themselves. Every day, the entrepreneur should set aside some time to think actively about this as well as other questions. For example: 'What can I do today to encourage my employees or assist management?', 'What special favour can I do for my customers?', 'How can I increase my personal efficiency?'

Group morale can be affected by several factors – for example, pleasant and safe working conditions, stress factors, working hours and wages. To secure positive group morale it is *vital* that staff who place the business' interests first and are motivated to attain its objectives and goals, are suitably rewarded or acknowledged. Most small businesses depend on the support of their employees to promote and sell their products and services to customers. Obviously, employees are much happier and better workers when they regard management as competent, fair, and aware of employees' contributions. Similarly, personnel expect to earn wages in relation to their contribution to the business, and often aspire to improved status. This may take the form of new job opportunities, participating in decision-making, or promotion.

SOWING THE SEEDS OF ENTHUSIASM

- *When you find yourself uninterested in something, apply yourself to the task and make a concerted effort to learn more about it.*
- *Broadcast good news.*
- *Develop a 'you are important' attitude. Be sincere at all times and remember names. People are inclined to do more for you when you make them feel important.*
- *Show appreciation for the things people do. Never miss an opportunity to congratulate someone on an achievement, or express sympathy in times of sorrow or disappointment.*
- *Cultivate the 'service first' attitude. Make it a rule in everything you do. Give people more than they expect to get.*

It is important that managers understand that most employees want to be recognized for their contribution to the business. Frustrations and a sense of insecurity arise when staff do not know how their tasks fit into the total operation, do not understand the value of the work they do, do not have anyone displaying interest in what they are doing, and do not know whether permanent employment is assured. *Regular feedback is essential.*

EMPLOYEE TAX AND BENEFITS

When a business employs staff, income tax, unemployment insurance and workmen's compensation is required (by law) to be paid on behalf of the employee. Additional employee benefits are regarded as voluntary and include medical aid/insurance and pension schemes. On registering with the Receiver of Revenue, employers must provide details of the business and the number of people on its pay-roll. When the employer pays employees, contributions to any pension or retirement annuity funds should be deducted from the employees gross earnings. Once these amounts have been subtracted, the deduction tables (issued by the Receiver of Revenue) will indicate the amount to be deducted as income tax. The employer is responsible for remitting the amount to the Receiver of Revenue. Employees may be taxed in one of two ways – either through Pay-As-You-Earn (PAYE), or Standard Income Tax on Employees (SITE). SITE accounts for an employee's final or minimum liability. It is not refundable except under certain limited circumstances where a re-determination may be made by the Receiver of Revenue.

UNEMPLOYMENT INSURANCE

Unemployment insurance is available to most employees. For this, the employer must register with the Department of Manpower. Business-owners are not eligible for unemployment benefits. Should an individual become unemployed, the system pays out a percentage of the final earnings received in a person's most recent job, but only for a limited period of time. It also provides funds for a contributor who becomes pregnant or ill, and for the dependants of a contributor who has died.

WORKMEN'S COMPENSATION

Workmen's compensation is available to all businesses registered with the Department of Inland Revenue, and provides for the payment of benefits to anyone injured as a result of his or her work responsibilities. Compensation is paid on temporary and permanent disablement, and to dependants in the event of death. Medical expenses may be paid for a limited period.

The employer must register with the Workmen's Compensation Commission. Registration forms are available from the Department of Manpower or by writing to the Commission. The Commissioner will assess the contribution the employer should make according to the annual wage bill paid by the business. The rate of contribution varies from industry to industry, but tends to be highest in the 'dangerous' industries which include mining, security services, transport and steel construction.

Business-owners are not eligible for Workmen's Compensation and are advised to contribute to a personal income protection plan.

CHAPTER

10

STRATEGIC PLANNING

■

WHERE AM I NOW?

WHERE AM I GOING?

HOW AM I GOING TO GET THERE?

■

Entrepreneurs operating successful businesses should recognize the importance of reassessing their situation on a regular basis. When business is good, it is easy to sit back and allow day-to-day operations to take their course. Proper and regular planning, however, is essential for the success and continued success of your business. Many entrepreneurs are lulled into complacency when business is prosperous, but this false sense of security has been known to cripple, and at times destroy, a business. No business, whether it is a micro-small business, or a giant conglomerate, is immune to this deception. Without a business plan a business may lose revenue, may not be prepared for an upswing or downturn in the economy, or changes in the particular industry.

It is ironic that entrepreneurs can devote years to planning a business, but once it is up and running, fail to see beyond the next business day. They forget that to maintain a strong position, they need to re-evaluate the business constantly in terms of products and services, consumer and marketing trends, economic and environmental changes, and that they may have to consider redefining certain goals. No business owner can assume that things will remain the same – all have to cope with change, be it driven by technology, the economy, customers or government regulations. Products and services also go through life cycles: introduction, growth, maturity, saturation and, eventually, decline. This means that a product has either reached a stage where it is obsolete or where the product must be re-evaluated and modified. In addition to reassessing the business plan, the owner-manager could update job descriptions for each employee.

Strategic planning is *essential*. It takes into account where you are now, where you are going, and how you can get there. It involves establishing goals and objectives, and mobilizing action.

When it comes to making product line changes, entrepreneurial companies have an advantage over large corporations as they have greater flexibility. They can identify new or changing needs sooner, and often implement their plans ahead of the competition. A periodic visit to competitors' operations can be to your advantage in developing product strategy.

Designing a strategic plan is not difficult or costly if it is incorporated in your day-to-day operations. By being alert to circumstances and dealing with problems and positive ideas as they occur, management and staff can make concrete decisions that alter and develop the 'strategic plan' to the benefit of the business as a whole. The plan should be tangible so that management and staff are able to work toward its goals. (Remember also, that poor money management can lead to a severe decline in the financial structure and operations of a business, lack of product development and diversification, and in some cases, bankruptcy.) For example, the entrepreneur cannot jump from one product line to another if it does not form part of the overall strategy. By altering the course of your business at random, you run the potential risk of over-spending funds allocated to operations, besides wasting time.

The easiest way to forge a strategic plan is to answer the following three questions: Where am I now? Where am I going? and How am I going to get there?

'WHERE AM I NOW?'

Take a long, hard look at your market – don't assume that your customers are the same as they have always been. Are you sure you still know what they want? Don't take it for granted that the answers are still relevant today.

What about your competition? Do you know what percentage of the market you serve and what percentage your competition serves? Has it changed over the year? Are aggressive competitors encroaching on your market? If so, why? After a careful appraisal of your market, conduct an internal survey to identify your business' strengths and weaknesses. How do you rate the standard of your manufacturing and marketing? How do you rate the quality of your sales force? You will find room for improvement in most areas.

'WHERE AM I GOING?'

Now it's time to plan for the future. If your business does not have a 'mission statement', now is the time to create one. It acts as a constant reminder and motivation to management and staff, as well as giving customers and shareholders the assurance that the promises stated will be met. A typical example would read something like this:

> The fundamental purpose of our company is to provide products and services of such quality that our customers will receive superior value; our employees and business associates will share in our success; and our stockholders will receive a sustained, superior return on their investment.

At this stage of your strategic plan you should also plan to take action to rejuvenate your product and service lines and, if need be, to switch to more profitable and promising commodities.

'HOW AM I GOING TO GET THERE?'

You have now reached the implementation stage of the analysis. Address the following questions:

- How will the business increase its profits, improve customer-relations, improve products, and explore new markets?
- If a competitor is moving into the market, how will you modify the product line and which marketing strategy will you use?

A strategic plan is only meaningful if it is integrated into the changing realities of your specific marketplace. Entrepreneurs must continually monitor the objectives and goals outlined in its 'strategic business plan', as well as industry trends and changing consumer tastes, sales volumes, costs, pricing, market trends, and related product considerations. The business owner must consider all this information to make accurate predictions about the direction the business is taking. Furthermore, entrepreneurs should remember that product decisions cannot occur in a vacuum and should encourage feedback from everyone involved in the business.

USEFUL ADDRESSES

ABSA (Head Office)
PO Box 7735
Johannesburg 2000
Tel: (011) 350-4000

Advice Bureau for Black Businessmen
Private Bag X5090
Pietersburg 0700

Afrikaanse-Handelsinstituut
PO Box 1741
Pretoria 0001

Amatola Finance Corporation
PO Box 8057
Nahoon 5201
Tel: (0431) 53-234
Fax: (0431) 53-949

Black Management Forum
6 Plein Street
Johannesburg 2001

Bochabela Finance Corporation (BFC)
PO Box 6407
Dunswart 1508
Tel: (011) 422-2022/8
Fax: (011) 54-2726

Bophuthatswana National Development Corporation
PO Box 11
Montshiwa
Bophuthatswana

Centre for Businessmen
University of Zululand
Private Bag X1001
Kwadlangezwa 3886

Centre for Developing Business
Wits Business School
PO Box 31170
Braamfontein 2017

Ciskei National Development Corporation
Private Bag 463
King William's Town 5600

Ciskei Small Business Development Corporation
PO Box 66
Bisho, Ciskei

Commerce and Tourism
Director-General Industries
Private Bag X84
Pretoria 0001

Decentralization Board
Private Bag X342
Pretoria 0001

Dept. of Trade and Industry
Registrar of Patents
Trade Marks
Designs and Copyright
Private Bag X406
Pretoria 0001
Tel: (012) 325-2350

Dir. of Export Promotion
Private Bag X84
Pretoria 0001

Eastern Transvaal Group Credit Company (ETC)
PO Box 53
Karino 1204
Tel: (01316) 84-0267

Eskom Finance Company (Pty) Limited (EFC)
PO Box 1091
Johannesburg 2000
Tel: (011) 800-8111
Fax: (011) 800-4642

Fabfin Development Foundation (FAB)
PO Box 269
Pretoria 0001
Tel: (012) 327-1940
Fax: (012) 327-1974

First National Bank Small Business Unit
PO Box 8785
Johannesburg 2000

Fort Hare Institute of Management
Private Bag X1314
Alice 5700

Get Ahead Foundation (GAF)
PO Box 3776
Pretoria 0001
Tel: (012) 342-3585/9
Fax: (012) 342-3596

Government Printers
Private Bag X85
Pretoria 0001
Tel: (012) 323-9331

Great North Credit Company (GNC)
PO Box 5788
Pietersburg 0700
Tel: (01521) 71-046
Fax: (01521) 74-392/912-630

Group Credit Company (GCC)
* PO Box 15545
Vlaeberg 8018
Tel: (021) 22-2840
Fax: (021) 24-3129
* PO Box 21962
Port Elizabeth 6000
Tel: (041) 56-3064
Fax: (041) 56-4851

Home Business Organization (HEWs)
PO Box 1051
Houghton 2041
Tel: (011) 487-1216

Institute for Small Business
University of the Western Cape
Private Bag X17
Bellville 7530

Institute of Independent Business
PO Box 84004
Greenside 2034
Tel: (011) 646-4617

Inst. of Inventors, Innovators Research and Development
PO Box 6191
Johannesburg 2000
Tel: (011) 648-6110

Kangwane Economic Development Corporation
PO Box 935
White River 1240

King Finance Company (KFC)
PO Box 6397
Bloemfontein 9300
Tel: (051) 47-4713/4
Fax: (051) 30-6965

Kwazulu Development Corporation
PO Box 2801
Durban 4000

Lebowa Development Corporation
PO Box 951
Pietersburg 0700

Masakhane Loan Services
PO Box 2801
Durban 4000
Tel: (031) 902-8955
Fax: (031) 902-4190

Metropolitan Housing Finance Co-operative (MET)
PO Box 1360
Pinegowrie 2123
Tel: (011) 789-6945
Fax: (011) 789-7298

Natal Credit Corporation (NCC)
Liberty Life House
Smith Street
Durban 4001
Tel: (031) 307-4877
Fax: (031) 305-1662

National Stokvel Association of South Africa (NAS)
PO Box 1595
Johannesburg 2000
Tel: (011) 788-4994
Fax: (011) 788-1050

Qwa-Qwa Development Corporation
PO Box 5063
Phuthaditjhaba 9866

Registrar of Companies and Close Corporations
PO Box 429
Pretoria 0001
Tel: (012) 325-2350

Rural Finance Facility (RFF)
PO Box 665
Johannesburg 2000
Tel: (011) 337-6208
Fax: (011) 333-3303

South African Bureau of Standards (SABS)
Private Bag X191
Pretoria 0001
Tel: (012) 428-7911
Fax: (012) 344-1568

Bloemfontein
Tel: (051) 47-4408
Cape Town
Tel: (021) 689-5511
Durban
Tel: (031) 28-9181
East London
Tel: (0431) 46-2351/2/3
Johannesburg
Tel: (011) 403-3940
Port Elizabeth
Tel: (041) 33-7748
Richard's Bay
Tel: (0351) 90-4091

South African Franchise Association
Private Bag 34
Auckland Park 2006

South African Institute of Patent Agents
PO Box 4685
Pretoria 0001
Tel: (012) 323-4315.

South African Transport Services (Transport Concessions)
Rates Section
Private Bag X47
Johannesburg 2000

SASOL (Transvaal) Dorpsgebiede Beperk (SAS)
PO Box 1
Secunda 2302
Tel: (0136) 40-3441
Fax: (0136) 40-3843

School of Business Leadership
University of South Africa
PO Box 392
Pretoria 0001

Shangaan / Tsonga Development Corporation
* Private Bag 401
Letaba 0870
* PO Box 559
Giyani 0826

Small Business Advisory Bureau
Potchefstroom University
PO Box 1880
Potchefstroom 2520

Small Business Advisory Services (Pty) Ltd
* PO Box 189
Stutterheim 4930
* PO Box 752
Isando 1600

SBDC
* PO Box 7780
Johannesburg 2000
Tel: (011) 643-7351
* PO Box 4295
Cape Town 8000
Tel: (021) 21-2480
* PO Box 1745
Port Elizabeth 6000
Tel: (041) 54-5494
Bloemfontein
Tel: (051) 478-380
Durban
Tel: (031) 33-7037/49

Nelspruit
Tel: (01311) 28-217/8
Pietersburg
Tel: (01521) 7-4357
Pretoria
Tel: (012) 26-8671/2
Soweto
Tel: (011) 949-0705

Small Enterprise Foundation (SEF)
Tel: (0152) 307-5837

Standard Bank Business Development Department
PO Box 62325
Marshalltown 2017

Transkei Small Industries Development Organization
PO Box 176
Umtata
Transkei

Trust Bank Bureau for Business / Management
PO Box 7694
Johannesburg 2000

Unit for the Development of Small Business
PO Box 1600
Port Elizabeth 6000

Unit for Entrepreneurship
Graduate School of Business
University of Pretoria
Pretoria 0001

Unit for Entrepreneurship and Small Business Management
Graduate School of Business
University of Stellenbosch
PO Box 610
Bellville 7530

Urban Foundation
PO Box 7694
Johannesburg 2000

Venda Development Corporation
PO Box 9
Sibasa 0970

Workmen's Compensation Commission
PO Box 955
Pretoria 0001
Tel: (012) 323-9911

Yskor Landgoed (Edms) Bpk (YLB)
PO Box 450
Pretoria 0001
Tel: (012) 298-2088
Fax: (012) 325-7155

BIBILIOGRAPHY

Bell, V, J Sloth-Nielson and J Housdon *Make More Money Part-Time* Struik Publishers, Cape Town, 1993.

Brits, RN and WD Rookie, *Marketing in South Africa* Macmillan, Johannesburg.

Clark, I and E Louw *Small Business Opportunities in South Africa* Struik Timmins Publishers, Cape Town, 1994.

Clark, I, E Louw and J Myburgh *More Small Business Opportunities in South Africa* Struik Publishers, Cape Town, 1993.

Divaris, C and ML Steyn *Old Mutual Income Tax Guide – the Do-It-Yourself Income Tax Manual.*

Du Plessis, F, WA Boonzaier, E Troost and JH Jordaan *Ways to Avoid Tax Legally* National Publishing, South Africa.

Hodgotts, RM and DF Kuratko *Effective Small Business Management*, Harcourt Brace Jovanovich Publishers.

Huxham, K and P Haupt *Income Tax* H&H Pulications, Cape Town.

Jordaan, J and M Heysteek *How to Plan for Your Retirement* Helderberg Publishers, Stellenbosch, 1993.

Lütge-Smith, T *Working from Home* Struik Publishers, Cape Town, 1993.

Lynas, MG and AP Dorrian *Managing the Smaller Firm – the South African Context* Southern Book Publishers, Johannesburg.

Macdonald, R and F Coffield *Risky Business* The Falmer Press, London.

Marsh, R *Business Success in South Africa* Struik Publishers, Cape Town, 1992.

Morris, R *Marketing to Black Townships – Practical Guidelines* Juta, Cape Town, 1992.

Olm, KW and GG Eddy *Entrepreneurship and Venture Management* Charles E Merrill Publishing Company.

Steinhoff, D and JF Burgess *Small Business Management Fundamentals* McGraw-Hill Book Company, New York.

Wright, C and B Phillips *Successful Small Business Management in South Africa* Struik Publishers, Cape Town, 1993.

INDEX